MathBrain
by BrainThink Learning

Authors:
Karen Kwan
Lynn Lim
Dr Tay Choo Chuan

PARTRIDGE

To order additional copies of this book, contact
Toll Free +65 3165 7531 (Singapore)
Toll Free +60 3 3099 4412 (Malaysia)
orders.singapore@partridgepublishing.com

www.partridgepublishing.com/singapore

To All Parents and Educators:

"I never teach my pupils.
I only attempt to provide the conditions in which they can learn."

—Albert Einstein

Contents

Acknowledgements

First and foremost, we would like to express our immense gratitude towards Kenneth Williams, a key contributor to this book; a respected figure, with over 40 years with Vedic Mathematics. We are truly honoured to feature his work – "Fun with Figures", from Chapter 9 to Chapter 12 of this book. After 27 years of studying, researching and teaching, Kenneth Williams founded the Vedic Mathematics Academy in 1998. He went on publishing articles, writing several books, creating DVDs and the growing popularity of his theory brought him to seminars and courses around the world.

Notable achievements include developing Tirthaji's material, left-to-right calculating, Astronomy, applications of Triples, extension of Tirthaji's 'Crowning Gem', and Calculus. More of his work can be explored on **https://www.vedicmaths.org**

This book would not have been a success without the efforts of Contributing Writers: Claire Grant, Christy Thoo; Contributing Reviewers and Editors: Goh Shuan Thing, Tan Chean Yen, Loh En Lin, Victoria Yong, Shirley Khor, Adlina A. Rahim and Lee Yan Ling. This book is a testament of their conscientious efforts in writing, reviewing and revising the content for it to be relatable and easily understood. Not to forget, we truly appreciate Ms Goh's creative infographic design input that brings the content to life. Only with their contributions can this book realise our vision of helping parents and educators alike understand and develop our children's learning experience today for limitless possibilities of tomorrow.

Author

Karen Kwan is an author, speaker, business coach, and the owner of 2 Children Education franchises, Math Monkey (Hong Kong) Limited and English Eagle (Hong Kong) Limited. She is also the Chairlady of two associations, Early Childhood Association and Asia Branding & Franchising Association. She is a mother of three daughters and was inspired by her daughters by chance. She begins to look for innovative ways to make children learn happily and effectively. She devotes herself to education and actively participates in different courses such as brain-based learning, high-level thinking, and so on. She also joins various professional coaches, such as Blair Singer, Robert Kiyosaki and Tony Robbins. She has a wide range of knowledge, and she practices them with her family and her business. Having been in the children education business for over ten years, she has participated vigorously and actively by being a mentor, speaker and lecturer for some renowned institutions.

Author

Lynn Lim, a proud mother of three young boys who started her working career as an accountant, but shortly decided to be a teacher and since then, has been passionately teaching young children for more than ten years at Math Monkey centres. Lynn loves playing with numbers and has been amazed by the principles of Vedic Math since 2008. She has been facilitating children to develop MathBrain with Vedic Math principles to solve problems. She believes that helping children learn the processes of problem-solving through understanding the logic behind an answer is as important as getting an answer quickly - which can be achieved with Vedic Math. With her interest and passion for educating children, and managing Math Monkey MathBrain centre in Penang on a full time basis, Lynn is able to manage her time to take care of her three young children aged 2, 4 and 6 years old. She has been a practitioner of BrainThink Learning principles at Math Monkey MathBrain Centre as well as with her children at home. Her young boys are trained to be independent, and she wishes to share her experience with other parents.

Author

Associate Professor Dr Tay Choo Chuan graduated with Bachelor of Science (Hons) in Mathematics, Master of Science (Quality and Productivity Improvement) and PhD in Mathematics from National University of Malaysia (UKM). The author has over 30 years of experience teaching in schools and university. He is currently attached to the Technical University of Malaysia in Melaka (UTeM) as an Associate Professor in Faculty of Electrical Engineering. He has published journal and conference papers, as well as supervising Master and PhD students on topics related to Mathematics. He has also authored over 20 Mathematics books.

CHAPTER 1

What Makes Learning Fun, Effective Yet Effortless

Introduction

Our children are growing up too fast. It feels like just yesterday that your child was just a baby and before you know it, it's already their first day of school. Do you find that your child is dreading school? That's not uncommon. Let's face it – we've been through this; as a young child, we'd definitely prefer playtime over memorising the timetable or doing countless math sums that we can't seem to get right.

Our children are learning more and faster than we can teach them, and the education system recognises the need to raise its standards to keep up consistently. Every child learns differently. Not every child thrives in a classroom environment. As parents, we want our children to be happy, but we also want them to do well; it stresses us out when our children dread school.

Have you been subconsciously asking yourself these questions?

- Is there a better way to help my child learn better?
- How can I help my child keep up with schoolwork effortlessly?
- Do I know my child well enough to improve their learning ability?
- How do I get my child to be motivated and enjoy learning?
- How can I make my child be as enthusiastic about learning as a fraction of how they feel when playing their favourite video game?
- I have tried everything I could think of, but nothing seemed to be working and my child still hates doing homework. What am I missing?

Well, for starters, you're missing an important aspect: **knowing and understanding your child.** Do you know your child's 5 Brain Abilities (5BA)?

Take the 5 Brain Abilities assessment today and identify your child's strengths and weaknesses. You may find information about the 5 Brain Abilities assessment by the end of chapter 8.

What can you learn from this chapter?

This chapter not only answers the above questions but also what learning, in today's context, demands from a child and how to bring the fun back into learning like any game a child looks forward to playing.

You will discover :

- The importance of moulding children through a positive learning approach
- That one size does not fit all, where learning goes beyond memorisation and repetition
- The power of resonance in learning
- That when children think, they learn
- That holistic education is the catalyst to positive child development

Holistic Learning vs Traditional Learning

Unfolding Children Through a Positive Learning Approach

"Children are not things to be molded, but are people to be unfolded."

—Jess Lair, author

Each child is unique; they all learn differently. Some children understand through diagrams and flowcharts, while others may require a verbal explanation before they understand. In the highly competitive education-based society of Asia, the academic debate on the best methods of learning continues.

Why Holistic Learning?

Holistic learning leads a child to fulfilment and self-actualisation.

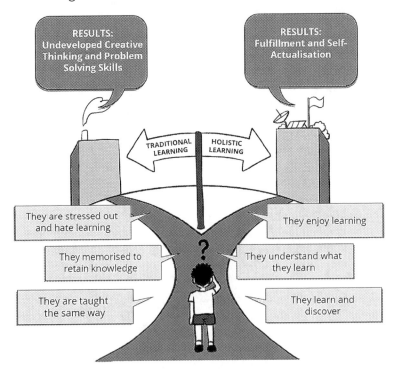

Exercise

What do you consider to be Traditional Learning?

List down what you think represents or describe Traditional Learning.

1) ....

2) ....

3) ....

4) ....

5) ....

How about Holistic Learning? Do you know what Holistic Learning means?

List down what you think Holistic Learning is.

1) ....

2) ....

3) ....

4) ....

5) ....

What is Holistic Learning?

Here are the three most important aspects of Holistic Learning.

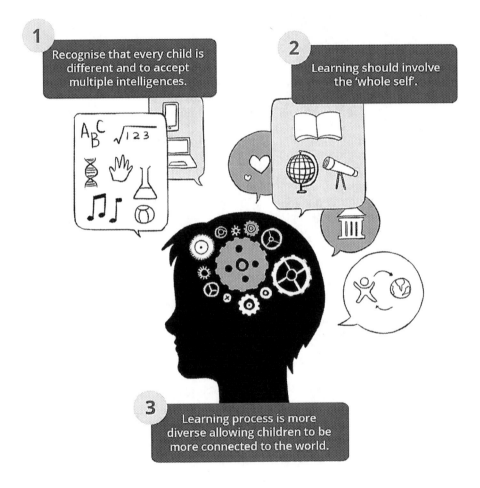

One Size Does Not Fit All

Parents and teachers shall accept and embrace their children's different types of intelligence, so they can engage more with the learning process to achieve better results.

In traditional education, often without realising, teachers use rote learning - a memorisation technique, as it seemed like the quickest learning method. Due to the lack of understanding, once the exam is over, students are very likely to forget the information they memorised.

Therefore, children without a good memory failed to perform academically. Memory should not be the primary indicator of intelligence. Instead, intelligence is linked to an interaction of prior knowledge with environmental factors and training.

Rote System

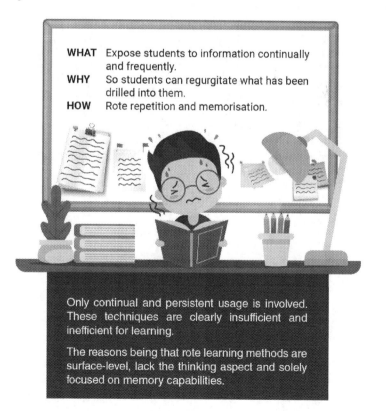

WHAT   Expose students to information continually and frequently.
WHY   So students can regurgitate what has been drilled into them.
HOW   Rote repetition and memorisation.

Only continual and persistent usage is involved. These techniques are clearly insufficient and inefficient for learning.

The reasons being that rote learning methods are surface-level, lack the thinking aspect and solely focused on memory capabilities.

Holistic Education

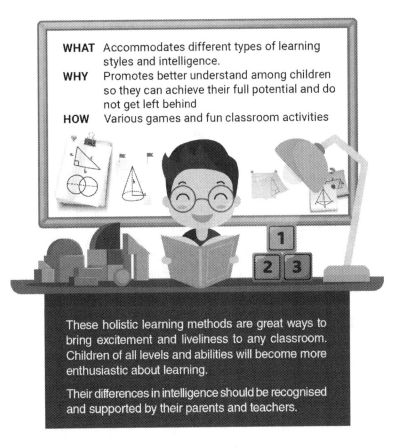

WHAT Accommodates different types of learning styles and intelligence.

WHY Promotes better understand among children so they can achieve their full potential and do not get left behind

HOW Various games and fun classroom activities

These holistic learning methods are great ways to bring excitement and liveliness to any classroom. Children of all levels and abilities will become more enthusiastic about learning.

Their differences in intelligence should be recognised and supported by their parents and teachers.

DID YOU KNOW? Finland and the Netherlands are known for the successful integration of holistic learning into their education systems from as early as nursery through university. With emotional development and creative thinking, it is no surprise that students in these countries do exceptionally well in both their academic and social lives.

Resonance Makes a Difference

When students solely memorise facts, they absorb information that is devoid of context, associations and meaning. As soon as students face unfamiliar or higher-order questions, they face great difficulty answering them.

However, students who practice holistic learning, gain a real understanding of knowledge. These students have formed meaningful connections with the information learned. The right understanding allows them to transfer knowledge efficiently and apply it where necessary.

When a student MEMORISES a fact   **When a student LEARNS a fact**

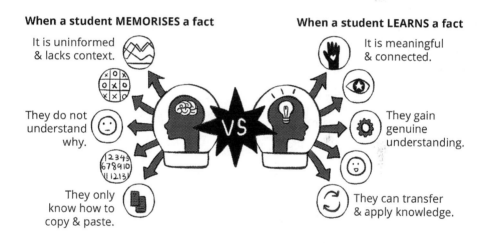

It is uninformed & lacks context.

They do not understand why.

They only know how to copy & paste.

It is meaningful & connected.

They gain genuine understanding.

They can transfer & apply knowledge.

Exercise

What do you imagine a Rote Learner's mind and a Holistic Learner's mind looks like? Illustrate the difference(s) you can think of below. Remember, there is no wrong or right answer.

Rote Learner's Mind

....

....

....

....

Holistic Learner's Mind

....

....

....

....

DID YOU KNOW? Most people perceive memorisation as a technique to learn. They are NOT synonymous. What distinguishes learning from memorisation is the sense of meaning. This is why memorised knowledge is not even half as useful as knowledge understanding.

When Children Think, They Learn

This statement may sound simple, but if a person uses proper thinking techniques, the learning can turn into a very fulfilling experience. Effective methods can change the learner's attitude and aptitude in their educational journey.

In most cases, the existing education system duly prepares all children to memorise information in order to ace the examinations, and then rely on average measurements and standardisations to measure intelligence — a system that not all individuals excel in.

Traditional Learning

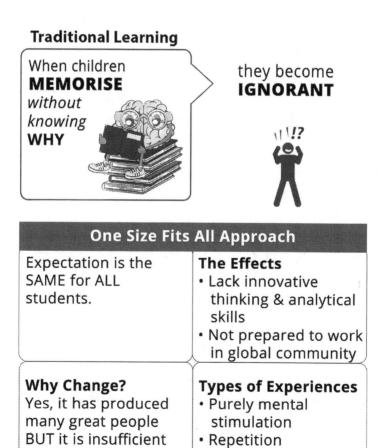

When children **MEMORISE** *without knowing* **WHY**

they become **IGNORANT**

One Size Fits All Approach	
Expectation is the SAME for ALL students.	**The Effects** • Lack innovative thinking & analytical skills • Not prepared to work in global community
Why Change? Yes, it has produced many great people BUT it is insufficient for the modern world.	**Types of Experiences** • Purely mental stimulation • Repetition • Memorisation

BrainThink Learning is an alternative methodology to rote learning, leading to enhanced retention and recollection. This method helps your child in preserving facts within their long-term memory, rather than only the short-term. We highly encourage children to immerse themselves into the world around them to discover the meaning and purpose of the knowledge they learn.

Brainthink Learning

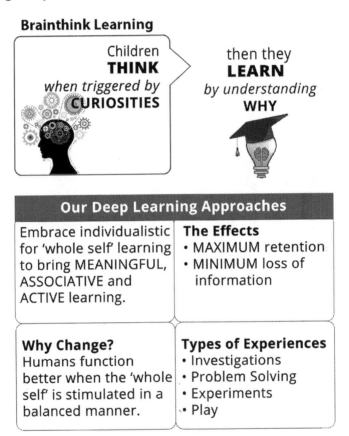

Children **THINK** *when triggered by* **CURIOSITIES**

then they **LEARN** *by understanding* **WHY**

Our Deep Learning Approaches	
Embrace individualistic for 'whole self' learning to bring MEANINGFUL, ASSOCIATIVE and ACTIVE learning.	**The Effects** • MAXIMUM retention • MINIMUM loss of information
Why Change? Humans function better when the 'whole self' is stimulated in a balanced manner.	**Types of Experiences** • Investigations • Problem Solving • Experiments • Play

DID YOU KNOW? There are various ways to find the same answer to a math problem. With **MathBrain** by **BrainThink Learning**, you will experience how math evolves into a process of logical discovery and thoughtful exploration, not just a memory process of getting the right answer.

Summary

Fulfilment and Self-Actualisation as One Moves Forward through Holistic Education

Play to learn

One of the philosophies behind holistic education is learning through playing, a method known to help your child to find out how to make sense of the world around them. Through self-directed play that inspires experiential learning, children can develop cognitive, social skills, as well as emotional maturity, which helps them gain the self-confidence needed to engage with new experiences and environments [i].

MathBrain program and the 5 Brain Abilities development are designed based on the philosophy of holistic education.

Holistic education as a catalyst for positive child development

* Would you like your children to have a deeper connection and appreciation of the extended world?
* Do you want to help them find their true talent and skill in an ever-increasing competitive and global society?

Holistic education can help mould our children of today into future leaders.

YOUR CHILDREN'S HOLISTIC LEARNING & 5 BRAIN ABILITIES DEVELOPMENT

START AT HOME

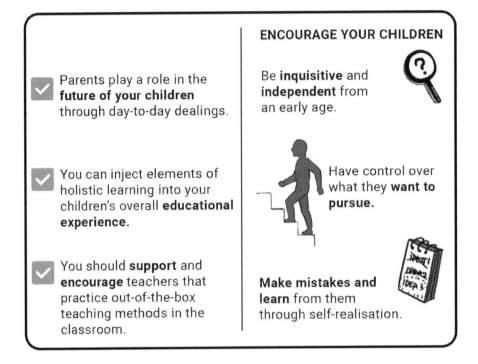

- Parents play a role in the **future of your children** through day-to-day dealings.

- You can inject elements of holistic learning into your children's overall **educational experience.**

- You should **support** and **encourage** teachers that practice out-of-the-box teaching methods in the classroom.

ENCOURAGE YOUR CHILDREN

Be **inquisitive** and **independent** from an early age.

Have control over what they **want to pursue.**

Make mistakes and learn from them through self-realisation.

CHAPTER 2

Why Some Children Perform Better Than Others: How Can I Guide My Child?

Introduction

"If the child is not learning the way you are teaching, then you must teach in the way the child learns."

—Rita Dunn

Problems tend to guide and educate us. Let's cultivate an environment where our children embrace problem-solving. Try solving the problems below:

1) **Peter has three apples. His mother gives him another two apples. How many apples does Peter have?**

   a. Is this a math question?

   b. If your child can read and is familiar with English words, but cannot answer this question, does your child face a math problem?

2) **3+2 = ?**

   a. Is this a math question?

   b. If your child cannot answer this question, does your child face a math problem?

   If your child can answer question (2), can read and is familiar with English words, but cannot answer question (1), what problem does the child have?

   Answer: **Cognitive Visualisation**

Mind-boggling, isn't it? What's going on? Well, don't worry. We are not here to test your knowledge. We wish to help you to understand your child better – know your child's 5 brain abilities and help them from young.

What can you learn from this chapter?

Once you understand the different areas of our brain that are being used to run our cognitive operations, you will then have better answers to the following topics in this chapter:

- Understand why some children perform better than others in exams
- Discover how proper brain training can help your child to overcome low performance in Math
- Learn essential parenting pointers and practical guidance on how to adopt a suitable attitude for a 'brain growth mindset' and create a home environment that naturally 'wires' your child's brain for performance
- A brief introduction to BrainThink Learning, educational programmes like MathBrain and how brain-based learning can help your child in cultivating brain growth

Learning is a Process Where Intelligence is Nurtured

"The best education does not happen at a desk, but rather engaged in everyday living—hands-on, exploring, in active relationship with life."

—Vince Gowmon

Our brain behaves like a muscle, and a child's brain can be trained to improve different cognitive functions like visualisation, memory, logical thinking or math skills.

However, many assume that possessing superior intelligence is a fixed condition. Rather than the lack of intelligence, it is a deficiency in proper brain development that will lead to the child's weaknesses in mathematical or problem-solving skills.

Parent's Common Misconception	**But, Intelligence Can Actually Be Nurtured**

• Intelligence is a fixed condition • My child is either 'smart' or not • They have fixed brain abilities • If my child failed in math, they are not a math person	• My child's brain can be continually trained to 'grow' • It grows at its own pace • Brain growth mindset can help my child to be a high achiever—in school or life

The belief of 'fixed intelligence' is contrasted with a brain growth mindset, where the brain is continually trained to grow gradually at its own pace. Moulding your child to have a brain growth mindset helps your child to be a high achiever, be it in school or life.

> ***DID YOU KNOW?*** Holistic learning methodologies like **BrainThink Learning** can counter the fixed intelligence viewpoint and improve low performance with effective brain learning strategies.

Performance and the Brain

"You cannot make people learn. You can only provide the right conditions for learning to happen."

—Vince Gowmon

Most children show the following similar pattern of brain development. The cerebral cortex is made up of nerve cells, neurons and axons that are densely packed in the outer layer of the brain.

Scientists have found that specific types of learning take place during this sensitive period of early childhood and the cortex is mostly responsible for the higher functions of the nervous system – such as learning, language, and memory [ii].

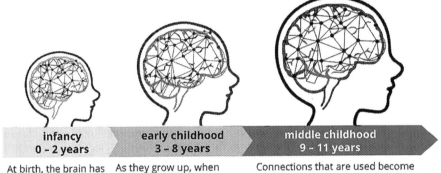

infancy 0 – 2 years	**early childhood** 3 – 8 years	**middle childhood** 9 – 11 years
At birth, the brain has 100 billion brain cells (called neurons).	As they grow up, when learning takes place, it strengthens the connections (called synapses) between the brain cells.	Connections that are used become permanent. If they are not stimulated early on, the connections will not develop. Thus, as they grow older, the unused connections will be 'removed'.

The brain grows rapidly during childhood. During which, learning strengthens the synapses making them permanent while unstimulated connections will die off. That is why this period of time is known as a child's golden age for learning.

DID YOU KNOW? A 15-year scientific study on brain development revealed that children who fared better in standard IQ tests had a brain cortex that is thicker and more matured.

We should not assume that thicker and more matured brain structure is genetically predestined.

- Our body's development is intimately linked to interactions with its environment.
- This suggests that those children who scored better tend to live in a vibrant social and linguistic environment.
- Detailed research suggests that thickness peaks after an average age of eight, for about four years.
- Therefore, intelligent children have a prolonged period of thickening in the prefrontal cortex.
- It gives them an extended period to develop the complex circuitry (or wiring) in their brain to support high-level thoughts.
- This means that there are no instant results; the more wiring needed, the longer it takes.

Another published study suggested that the brain is highly malleable. There are no particular interventions that might boost a child's intelligence, but experience and environmental cues play a crucial role in shaping it. It can be trained to do so by exposing your child to different environments [iii].

Conditioning

- Much of brain growth pattern is due to the environment that surrounds your child.
- It is the type of 'stimulation' the brain receives and the conditioning it is exposed to.
- This suggests that a child could be a low achiever due to the lack of environmental interactions they have been subjected to.
- Therefore, an inappropriate approach will mean that the brain is not allowed to develop to its full potential.

Fixed Intelligence vs Brain Growth

"If everything was perfect, you would never learn and you would never grow."

– Beyoncé Knowles

Children raised to uphold a proud **fixed mindset** of their own intelligence:
- are usually concerned about their image to look 'smart'
- makes actual learning process a second priority
- often have a negative view of others who put in a lot of effort in a particular task
- believe that having to exert more/hard work at something is an indication of a low ability

Children with a **growth mindset**:

- recognise that everyone makes mistakes even successful entrepreneurs, elders, and themselves included
- they are not preoccupied with their own intelligence
- they know they can learn and rise above their mistakes

Over 35 years of scientific investigation suggests that if we overstress on intellect and 'winning', we'll make our children:

- More vulnerable to failure
- Fearful of challenges
- Unable to deal with mistakes
- Unwilling to overcome their shortcomings

You need to support your children in making mistakes

Mistakes grow the brain. A brain growth mindset allows children to be curious, try new things, fail and then go on until they overcome the error. They will learn and grow up confidently!

How to Stimulate Your Child's Brain

"All children have within them the potential to be great kids. It's our job to create a world where this potential can flourish."

—Stanley Greenspan

Ways to create appropriate environments for nurturing your child's brain-growth mindset.

1. Let them make mistakes and learn from them

An essential part of intelligence is the awareness of what to do **after** having made a mistake. Hence, teaching the children that it is alright to make mistakes can change the entire trajectory of their mindset positively.

What you can do:

- Don't let your child be afraid of making mistakes.
- Don't leap in to correct their mistakes.
- Give them the opportunity to figure out their own mistakes and learn from them.

2. Nurture positive behaviours in them with your positive actions

Studies reveal that the area of the brain responsible for cognitive control reacts strongly to positive feedback at that age, but hardly at all to negative feedback. Positive behaviours help your child to identify the goodness.

What you can do:

Nurture positive behaviours through your thoughts, words, and actions to build your child's brain growth mindset.

3. Reward them for being good—Be firm, fair, friendly

School children often spend most of their day being told what to do or what they are doing wrong. They need to be praised for good efforts at home. Focus on your child's effort, not just their grades and deliver consequences with empathy.

What you can do:

- Reward your child regularly for any good effort, even for minor tasks.
- Tell your child what you want rather than what you do not.
- Follow the 3 'F's' of parenting - Be Firm, Be Fair, Be Friendly.

4. Provide clear communication to your child

Before you shout, learn simple skills to ensure that you have your child's attention. Poor listeners often live in a noisy or auditory stimulating environment. This is much more apparent in today's society, where devices and extraneous background noises surround us.

What you can do:

- Create a low-conflict, collaborative environment.
- Get down to your child's level and make good eye contact.
- In a clear, calm voice, tell them what is required of them.
- Keep instructions short and simple.
- Ask them to repeat your instructions.
- Congratulate your child when they complete each step.
- Give a few instructions at a time.

5. Help them find the right friends

Cultivating openness to meeting new people and befriending other children besides their cousins or siblings can bring positive influence on your child's development. Not only does this widen your child's social circle, but it also improves their communication skills and integration into a community.

What you can do:

- Start with neighbours or like-minded acquaintances from school.
- Introduce a few friends at a time.
- Observe how your children interact around them.
- Always avoid aggressive physical behaviours.

6. Let your children be bored

Technology can be seen as a parent's best friend if you are looking for a convenient distraction or a 'virtual babysitter' to keep your child occupied. Unfortunately, it provides minimal brain growth development and rather, quickens the pace of wasted neural connections elimination.

What you can do:

- Don't let your child be seated stationary in front of the TV.
- Be selective about the technology your child uses.
- Know the positive and negative effects of technology.
- Let them be bored so they can enjoy a "quiet reflection".

Summary

Creating the Appropriate Attitude and Environment to Nurture a Brain Growth Mindset

Putting proper brain training into practice

It is not the lack of intelligence, but a deficiency in proper brain training that leads to the child's mistakes in math problems.

BrainThink Learning is one of the holistic learning methods that provide such training to counter the fixed intelligence viewpoint and improve poor performance with effective brain-based learning strategies.

THE 6 STEPPING STONES TO A BRAIN GROWTH MINDSET

Mistakes grow your child's brain as they learn a great deal from them.

1.

Positive actions encourage your child to be more receptive and open.

2.

Reward your child with the 3Fs in mind—be Firm, Fair & Friendly.

3.

Let your child be bored. **Inaction** teaches them to enjoy 'quiet reflection'.

6.

Get **attention** from your child by going down to their level and making eye contact.

4.

Surround your child with **friends** who will be of good influence.

5.

Developing a brain growth mindset and positive parent-child relationships

Active learning educational programmes like MathBrain are designed to make children excited and curious about playing games and lead them to learn math in fun ways. Parents can learn and create such a programme at home to foster positive parent-child relationships.

Do you want your child to begin developing a 'growth mindset' and an agile mind capable of making the best choices? Our programmes and recommended approaches can help you get involved in the development of your child's 5 brain abilities.

CHAPTER 3

How Can The 5 Brain Abilities Make My Child Smarter?

Introduction

Have you ever wondered about your children's brain abilities? We've talked about the differences every child has and how you can create a conducive learning environment for them—especially at the speed of which they are absorbing information and learning today.

Next, we'd like to talk about your child's 5 Brain Abilities (5BA). I'm sure you'd have questions like:

- What are the 5 brain abilities and how do they play a role in learning?
- Is it sufficient to be activating just a few of these abilities? Will it have an impact on cognitive performance?
- How can you tap into the brain abilities?
- Is it possible to nurture and utilise all 5 brain abilities and benefit from them?
- What are the steps to engage 5 brain abilities in solving problems?
- Do you want your child to develop inner motivation and learn out of self-interest?
- Would you like to see your child become a confident learner?
- How do I help or guide my child to be a brain-based learner?

What can you learn from this chapter?

We want to guide you and enable you to find the answers to the questions you have on the 5BA. This chapter will help you discover:

- About 5 Brain Abilities (5BA) and their significance in a child's learning and problem-solving capabilities
- Learn how and why you need to identify your child's 5BA
- How to challenge your child to mould them into future leaders
- 5BA in the BrainThink Learning Environment with Play to Learn Approach
- Recommended day-to-day activities for developing and enhancing your child's Brain Abilities
- How the brain functions
- Ways to further improve your child's Brain Abilities
- 7 Power tips to boost brainpower

Exercise

Before we get into the details, we would like you to think about the following carefully. Don't worry about the answers. We are not here to test your knowledge. These questions are meant to help you understand how to guide your child better.

Part 1

We have red balls in 1 basket and white balls in another basket. We want to find out how many red balls and white balls there are.

2 equations:

1) If we take 1 red ball and 1 white ball out from the baskets each time, eventually, red ball basket will be empty, and there will be 50 white balls left in the other basket.

2) If we take 1 red ball and 3 white balls out from the baskets each time, eventually, the white ball basket will be empty, and there are 50 red balls left in the other basket.

Questions:

1) Can you figure out the number of red and white balls?

   (Do not use algebra as this question was used in a book published in Singapore for primary school). Guess: What age group was this question targeting?

2) Is this a math question?

3) Can you use your memory or any formula to find the answer to this question?

4) What brain abilities does a person need to figure out such a question?

5) How many times did your brain "process" to:
- Work out the solution?
- Gather accurate information?
- Understand the relationship between the numbers in the equations?
- Try to figure out various ways to find the answer?
- Try to apply an appropriate formula to find the answer?

6) Did your brain:
- **Explore** possible ways to find the answer?
- **Test** if the possible answer is correct?
- **Repeat** with the possible ways and Test it again to see if you can find the answer?

Part 2

> **Which brain ability is the most important for solving problems?**
>
> * It is universal that brain memory and processing speed are essential but how important are they?

Questions:

1) Is **brain memory** or **processing speed** the most important ability for solving problems?

2) Everyone has 5 major brain abilities:

   Memory, Processing Speed, Logical Thinking, Attention, Visualisation (cognitive).

3) For the brain abilities above, please list your level of familiarity with each of the concepts:

Most familiar: 1. _____ 2. _____

3. _____ 4. _____

Least familiar: 5. _____

4) Problem-solving process.

   When we try to solve a problem, we need to gather information/data (input) to understand the problem. Then, we process it to find the answer (output).

   Input ⟶ Process ⟶ Output

5) Do you know which brain ability functions at the input, process, and output stages?

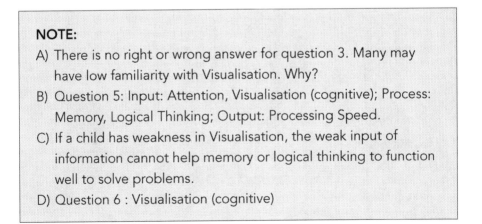

Stage	Brain Ability
Input	_____
	_____
Process	_____
	_____
Output	_____

6) Which brain ability is vital to building confidence before solving a problem?

NOTE:

A) There is no right or wrong answer for question 3. Many may have low familiarity with Visualisation. Why?

B) Question 5: Input: Attention, Visualisation (cognitive); Process: Memory, Logical Thinking; Output: Processing Speed.

C) If a child has weakness in Visualisation, the weak input of information cannot help memory or logical thinking to function well to solve problems.

D) Question 6 : Visualisation (cognitive)

The 5 Great Abilities Your Brain Possesses

Your child's learning process and problem-solving capability have much to do with their brain's abilities. These abilities (or cognitive abilities) are attention, visualisation, logical reasoning, memory and processing speed. Within every child lies the 5 great brain abilities that can be sharpened to enhance their learning and to realise their potential.

What are the functions of these abilities? How can they benefit your child's learning when applied?

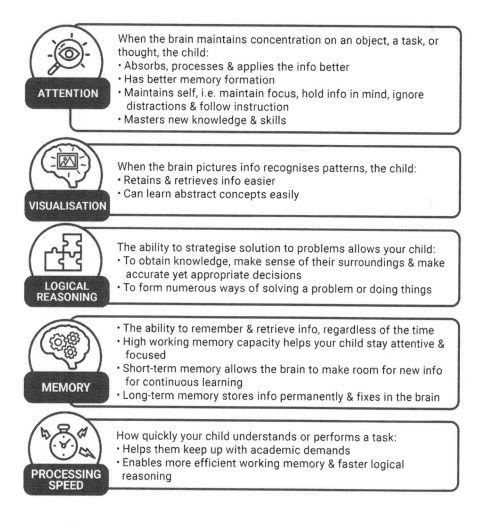

ATTENTION

When the brain maintains concentration on an object, a task, or thought, the child:
- Absorbs, processes & applies the info better
- Has better memory formation
- Maintains self, i.e. maintain focus, hold info in mind, ignore distractions & follow instruction
- Masters new knowledge & skills

VISUALISATION

When the brain pictures info recognises patterns, the child:
- Retains & retrieves info easier
- Can learn abstract concepts easily

LOGICAL REASONING

The ability to strategise solution to problems allows your child:
- To obtain knowledge, make sense of their surroundings & make accurate yet appropriate decisions
- To form numerous ways of solving a problem or doing things

MEMORY

- The ability to remember & retrieve info, regardless of the time
- High working memory capacity helps your child stay attentive & focused
- Short-term memory allows the brain to make room for new info for continuous learning
- Long-term memory stores info permanently & fixes in the brain

PROCESSING SPEED

How quickly your child understands or performs a task:
- Helps them keep up with academic demands
- Enables more efficient working memory & faster logical reasoning

No single brain ability is better or more crucial to your child's learning and development than another. When all five capabilities are given equal emphasis and are exercised, your child will be able to develop their abilities fully.

DID YOU KNOW? MathBrain can be developed and designed to ensure the brain abilities complement each other, working hand-in-hand throughout the learning process.

Why You Need to Know Your Child's 5 Brain Abilities

What you do or don't, will have a lasting impact on your child's brain abilities and development. However, many parents are not making the most of simple, vital opportunities to stimulate full and healthy growth during their child's early years.

The answer to it is simply *play*. However, in Asian culture, *play* is a taboo. We'll talk more about that as we dive deeper into the topic.

How do I know my child's 5 Brain Abilities?

Having learnt that it takes all 5 Brain Abilities to optimise your child's development, surely you would like to know what you can do as parents, teachers or caretaker, to hone these abilities in your child. The 5 Brain Abilities Assessment (5BA Assessment) is a tool for you to learn about your child's abilities, which we will elaborate more in Chapter 8.

In the following pages, you will learn:

- The right approach to positively guide children to start on a journey of exploration
- Everyday activities you can do with your child to encourage brain abilities' development
- The functions of the brain
- Tips for improving your child's brain abilities

Challenges Ahead!

Did you expect this segment to be something about working with challenging behaviours? Not quite so. The pace of the world today is very different from the past. Today's children have access to much more information from various sources and are learning at a quicker pace. They always feel the need to do something, are curious about their world or continuously need a new challenge, which is good if you have the know-how to deal with such needs.

Challenge Children and Mould Them into Future Leaders

With BrainThink Learning methodology, your child's potential will be drawn out. Your child becomes an active learner, able to gather and process information, and apply logic and creativity in the use of their knowledge. They will also design solutions to help them solve problems.

5 Brain Abilities in the BrainThink Learning Environment with Play to Learn Approach

BrainThink Learning Environment: a positive atmosphere with diverse learning opportunities, engaging and stimulating materials that help shape a child into a holistic and active learner.

Using their **5 Brain Abilities,** a child can efficiently absorb most, if not all, critical points in a lesson through various stimulations and activities, enriching games, and active play that engages their whole self.

This is what the natural "play and learn" process does:

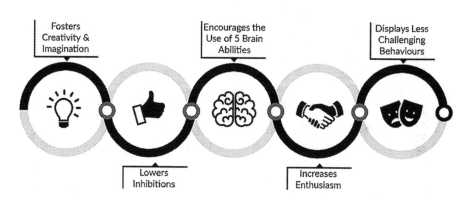

| Fosters Creativity & Imagination | Encourages the Use of 5 Brain Abilities | Displays Less Challenging Behaviours |

| Lowers Inhibitions | Increases Enthusiasm |

DID YOU KNOW? The **BrainThink Learning** environment fosters creativity, fun, and consequently nurtures a child's active learning process. This induces more positive behaviours from children when contrasted against traditional instruction-based teaching.

Everyday Activities You Can Do with Your Child to Encourage Brain Abilities' Development

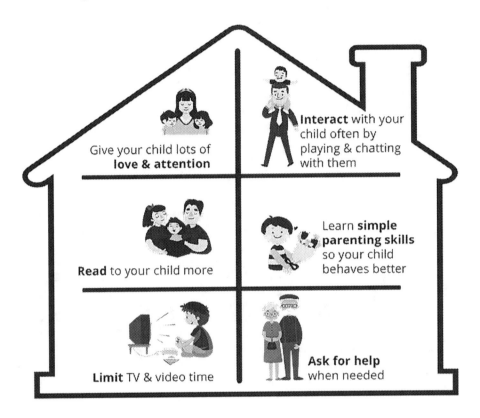

- Provide your child with lots of love and attention. No matter what a child's age, holding, hugging and listening are meaningful ways to show your child they matter.
- Interact with your child often by chatting, playing, and singing with them. Your child will grow up feeling special and important to you. You will also learn a lot about your child's interests and skills.
- Read to your child more. Research has shown that children who grew up being told stories every day have a more extensive vocabulary than other children. Reading also provides children with new perspectives about the world we live in.

- Learn some simple parenting skills to let your child exhibit desired behaviours. The most important parenting trait is to be consistent – in rewarding favourable behaviours, you want to see your child do more of, and meting out consequences for misbehaviours.
- Limit your child's television and video time to no more than 1-2 hours of educational viewing per day.
- Ask for help when you need it from your spouse, family, or anyone you can trust your child with. Parenting is wonderful, but hardly easy when done alone.

Brain Functions

Children's brain functions develop from the time they are born:

1. Infancy: A newborn has enough motor control to feed and to move away from painful or other unpleasant stimuli

2. Toddlerhood: auditory and visual skills improve during this time.

3.Preschool : Children learn how to coordinate fine motor and visual skills. They are able to copy letters, figures and actions they see.

4.Early elementary year : Children learn both academically and socially. reading, maths, and writing skills become more developed

5.Middle school year : In schools, more emphasis on inferential learning, and less on rote learning. Learning becomes more consolidated, as it is stored in the long term memory

How to Improve Children's Brain Abilities

"The potential of the human mind is subject to, and limited only by, our individual beliefs or unbelief as to whether we can accomplish a thing or not."

—Chuck Danes

Tips and Exercises to Sharpen and Boost Your Child's Brainpower

Strong brain abilities depend on the health and vitality of a child's brain. There are lots of things that can be done to boost a child's brain abilities. Read on to learn more about the 7 tips that will add up to a brainier you.

The 7 Power Tips to Boost Brainpower

Think of something new you have always desired to try, like pottery, speaking French, ballroom dancing, or solving mathematical puzzles. Any of these activities can help to boost a child's brain abilities, as long as they're occupied in tackling challenges.

Four Key Elements of a Good Brain-Boosting Activity

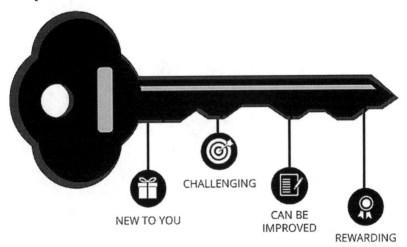

NEW TO YOU

CHALLENGING

CAN BE
IMPROVED

REWARDING

Improving Brainpower Abilities

Tip #1: Best Brain Exercise – Keep Learning New Things

Continually Exercise Your Brain to Improve the Brainpower Abilities

1. The best brain exercise **break routines** and **challenge** children to use and develop new brain pathways.

2. **Keep Learning.** Whether children learn from reading books or by visiting new places, the important thing is that the child's brain is always working to store new information.

3. Experts recommend that you **challenge your mind regularly** with Maths, puzzles, music, art, and other stimulating activities.

4. **Brain fitness exercises** build up a child's brain and at the same time, maintain top brain health.

Tip #2: Regular Physical Exercise – A Fit Body is also a Fit Mind

In general, anything good for children's hearts are excellent for their brains! Physical exercise plays a significant role in mental health. It helps children's minds stay sharp and reduce stress. For children, exercise means playing and being physically active, this can happen anywhere from gym class, during recess, at dance class or soccer practice!

BRAIN - BOOSTING EXERCISE TIPS

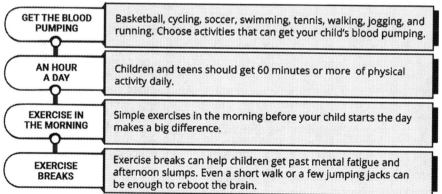

GET THE BLOOD PUMPING	Basketball, cycling, soccer, swimming, tennis, walking, jogging, and running. Choose activities that can get your child's blood pumping.
AN HOUR A DAY	Children and teens should get 60 minutes or more of physical activity daily.
EXERCISE IN THE MORNING	Simple exercises in the morning before your child starts the day makes a big difference.
EXERCISE BREAKS	Exercise breaks can help children get past mental fatigue and afternoon slumps. Even a short walk or a few jumping jacks can be enough to reboot the brain.

Tip #3: Get Sufficient Sleep

As cliché as it sounds, getting sufficient sleep should be made a priority. Skimping a few hours of sleep each day makes a big difference – you compromise your attention, visualisation, logical thinking, memory, and processing speed all at once.

- **Pre-schoolers: Typically sleep 11 to 13 hours each night.** With further development of imagination, pre-schoolers commonly experience nightmares. Also, sleepwalking and night terrors peak during the pre-school years.

- **Children aged 5 to 12: Need 10 to 11 hours of sleep each night.** At this age, more time is spent on extracurricular activities in school, sports, and school-aged children become more interested in TV, computers, and the Internet, and also caffeinated products. These can lead to difficulty falling asleep, nightmares and disruptions to their sleep. In particular, watching TV too close to bedtime has been associated with bedtime resistance; trouble falling asleep, anxiety around sleep, and resulting in sleeping fewer hours.

Signs of Sleep Deficit

- **Mood:** Your child may be moody, irritable, and cranky. In addition, they may have a difficult time regulating their mood, and thus may get frustrated or upset more easily.

- **Behaviour:** Your child is more likely to have behaviour issues, such as noncompliance, cognitive problems, and hyperactivity.

- **Cognitive ability:** Your child may have problems with attention, memory, decision-making, reaction time, and creativity, which are vital for brain development.

Sleeping Tips

· **Go to bed** at the **same time** every night and **get up** at the **same time** each morning.

· Have a **relaxing bedtime routine** that ends in the room where the child sleeps.

· **Avoid all screens** for at least an hour before bed.

· Your child should sleep in the **same sleeping environment** every night, in a room that is cool, quiet and dark – and without a TV.

· **Cut** back on **caffeine.**

Tip #4: Make Time for Friends/Healthy Relationships

Humans are highly sociable animals. We are not meant to survive, let alone thrive, in isolation. Interaction with friends stimulates the best kind of brain exercise for children, training their soft skills and people skills.

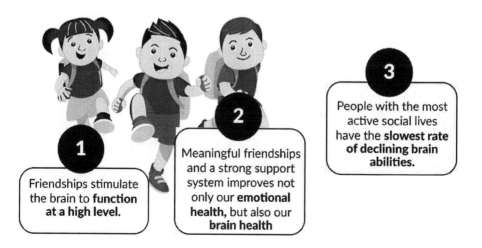

1
Friendships stimulate the brain to **function at a high level.**

2
Meaningful friendships and a strong support system improves not only our **emotional health,** but also our **brain health**

3
People with the most active social lives have the **slowest rate of declining brain abilities.**

Tip #5: Play and Have Fun!

Playing is essential to the brain's development because it contributes to the cognitive, physical, social, and emotional well-being of children. It also offers an ideal opportunity for parents to engage with their children. Playing and having fun establishes new neural connections, allowing the children to be more intelligent. It improves the ability to perceive others' emotional state and to adapt to ever-changing circumstances. Not only that, the periods of most rapid brain growth frequently involves play.

Essential Dimensions of Play for Children

- Voluntary, enjoyable, purposeful and spontaneous
- Creativity expanded using problem solving, social, language and physical skills
- Helps expand on new ideas
- Helps the child to adapt socially
- Helps to prevent emotional problems

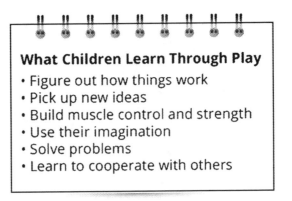

What Children Learn Through Play
- Figure out how things work
- Pick up new ideas
- Build muscle control and strength
- Use their imagination
- Solve problems
- Learn to cooperate with others

Tip #6: Eat a Brain-Boosting Diet

A child's brain needs the energy to stay alert in continuous learning and to help attain their brain's full functioning ability. A healthy diet gives children's minds the fuel required to run correctly. Just as the body needs fuel, so does the brain.

The following nutritional tips will help boost your child's brainpower.

BOOST YOUR CHILDREN'S BRAIN WITH FOOD

1 EAT THESE FOODS

Eggs: They contain the essential brain-building nutrient, choline.

Omega 3 fatty acid-rich foods: Salmon, tuna, avocado, flaxseed oils, chia seed, almonds and walnuts.

Wholegrain Food: Contains lots of Vitamin B that help enhance memory retention & recall abilities in children.

Apples & Plums: Lunchbox-friendly, contain quercetin, an antioxidant that may fight decline in mental skills.

2 AIM FOR LOW GI

GI (Glycaemic Index) is the measurement carried out on carbohydrate-containing foods and their impact on our blood sugar.

Children's brains need **long-lasting energy** to get through a day of learning and playing.

Low-GI food keeps blood sugar levels in check and slowly release energy into the body as glucose, which the brain then uses as a fuel.

3 BREAKFAST IS ESSENTIAL

Several studies shown that **skipping breakfast** results in **reduced learning, reduced attention, and poor food choices** for the rest of the day. Therefore, never start a child's day without any food intake.

4 AVOID JUNK FOOD

Junk food and fast food can **negatively affect a child's brainpower**. A study found that eating high levels of **"bad fats"** like trans-fatty acids could clog up the brain and interfere with the way it sends messages hence, **affecting learning**.

Tip #7: Identify and Treat Children's Brain Problems

Diagnosing a learning disability is a lengthy process. It involves undergoing numerous tests, evaluation of medical history, and further observation by a trained specialist. It is essential to obtain a referral by a professional. Start with your child's school; and if they are unable to help, then seek advice from doctors, friends or family who have successfully dealt with learning disabilities.

Common Types of Brain Disabilities for Kids

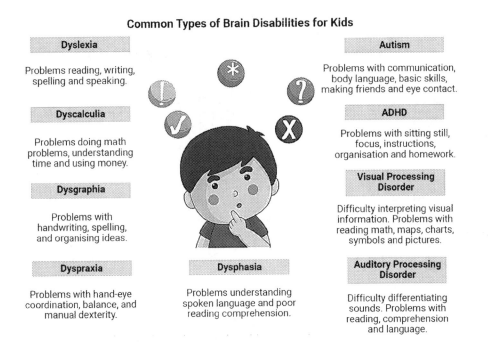

Dyslexia
Problems reading, writing, spelling and speaking.

Dyscalculia
Problems doing math problems, understanding time and using money.

Dysgraphia
Problems with handwriting, spelling, and organising ideas.

Dyspraxia
Problems with hand-eye coordination, balance, and manual dexterity.

Dysphasia
Problems understanding spoken language and poor reading comprehension.

Autism
Problems with communication, body language, basic skills, making friends and eye contact.

ADHD
Problems with sitting still, focus, instructions, organisation and homework.

Visual Processing Disorder
Difficulty interpreting visual information. Problems with reading math, maps, charts, symbols and pictures.

Auditory Processing Disorder
Difficulty differentiating sounds. Problems with reading, comprehension and language.

Types of specialists who may be able to test for and diagnose learning disabilities include:

- Clinical psychologists
- School psychologists
- Child psychiatrists
- Educational psychologists
- Developmental psychologists
- Occupational therapists (test sensory disorders that can lead to learning problems)
- Speech and language therapists

Summary

It takes Teamwork from Both Internal and External Factors

Putting our focus on just one or two brain abilities is insufficient. As we have come to learn – the way our brain functions teach us that we need to harmoniously develop all our brain abilities internally to optimise learning and simultaneously, have an equally harmonious external team working towards developing a whole child.

How to Create Internal and External Harmony to Improve Your Child's 5 Brain Abilities

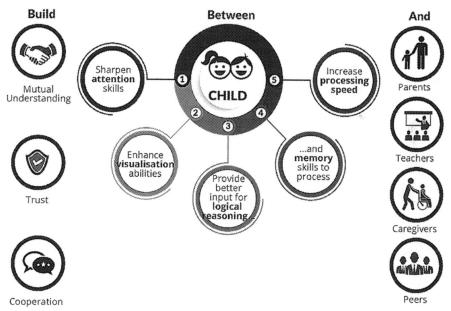

Learning is a constant process. There is no right or wrong because education is a journey; it was never just about the destination.

Being mindful of the definition of education is essential; as it will result in how it is pursued, as well as the principles we have in pursuing those goals.

Fundamentally, when we have the right priorities and understanding, we can, and will be the change that we are looking for in our learning evolution. As for how it is with the 5 Brain Abilities, utilising the right abilities enables us to solve problems in a new light—using accurate and sensible, yet creative and innovative ways in designing solutions, and in creating new paradigms in our minds.

CHAPTER 4

Play-To-Learn & Developing The 5 Brain Abilities

Introduction

Do you know that the more versatile you are, the more adaptable you will be in life? Playing has many benefits. However, many Asian parents see playtime as a distraction to education, which is misconceived. Children, in fact, pay more attention to academic tasks when they are given frequent, brief opportunities for free play [iv].

To navigate our ever-changing world, play should be encouraged in our children to pick up and develop their adaptability towards behaviour, cognitive ability, creativity and emotions.

We have so far discussed the 5 Brain Abilities (5BA), which are **Attention, Visualisation (cognitive), Logical Thinking, Memory and Processing Speed.** These abilities play a vital role in their learning, confidence and problem-solving capabilities.

What can you learn from this chapter?

We will talk about the strategies and learning practises parents can use to help their child exercise each cognitive function. As you go through this chapter, you will discover why more Active Players with inner motivation towards learning are needed and how these qualities can be nurtured within.

You will learn:

- What is truly needed but not practised actively
- The importance of Active Play
- Play-based learning games you can use for your child to develop their 5BA: Child-focused Games for Attention Games, Get the Best out of Play for Visualisation Games, Beyond Grades for Logical Reasoning Games, Fun with Memory for Memory Games, The Speed Factor for Processing Speed Games

---

The Need of the Hour

We know that the development of the 5 Brain Abilities (5BA) is crucial to your child's learning. Unfortunately, they tend to be given less-than-required attention in formal education.

The MathBrain program aims to change that with:

√ A supplementary and more direct approach to a child's scholastic development by focusing on the 5 Brain Abilities.
√ A streamlined programme to develop cognitive skills, aimed at improving mental performance in solving mathematical problems

What is Play-based Learning?

√ One of the prevalent techniques
√ Method to engage your child with their own natural motivation
√ Based on the philosophy that when children are playing, they learn.

Active Play

Play aids understanding and long-term memory learning that memorisation is incapable of emulating.

√ Every child has an intrinsic desire to engage in types of play based on their interests and strengths.
√ Children learn much through play.
√ Play-based learning allows children to explore, discover, negotiate, take risks, create meaning and solve problems.

Unfortunately, play-based methods are less understood and perceived as a leisure activity rather than academic in most parents' point of view. In fact, play-based learning is a complex form of natural enquiry that requires knowledge about the child's emerging strengths and interests.

More importantly, it leads to long-term memory fixation in a way that trumps memorisation any day.

The Game Master Knows the Best Games for its Players

Natural motivation has much to do with mental games. Taking cues from your child's intrinsic motivation, as a parent, you can:

√ recognise teachable moments as they occur during play
√ gently guide your children towards specific games based on your child's natural interests

Let us take an in-depth look at different play-based games that target specific cognitive abilities and are instrumental in strengthening mental capacity.

Types of Mental Games You Can Use to Help Your Child Develop Their 5 Brain Abilities

1. ATTENTION GAMES	
• Your child can focus their concentration for extended periods of time. • In our modern age of technology, even children without ADHD (attention deficit or hyperactivity) disorders, find it difficult to concentrate on a single task for an extended duration	**Child-focus Games** **Steps:** 1) Identify an activity that your child is particularly interested in. 2) Encourage your child to focus on it longer. 3) Provide creative input and get involved in the activity with them. **Example:** If the task is Lego building or making something, ask them to describe what they are doing. Show interest, be involved and encourage them to keep going. Give them a reward that can thrill them! **Why:** Your involvement plays a significant role in their engagement. This makes it harder for the child to be distracted if their mind is entirely on the task. Just like learning a musical instrument, the amount of engagement required to train their attention.

2. VISUALISATION GAMES

- Your child's brain can visualise information and recognise patterns.
- Making learning "visible", either through audio-visual materials or imagination are common forms of stimulating visualisation.

Get the Best Out of Play

Steps:

If your child has difficulty explaining something or is quiet:

1. Encourage your child to draw to express themselves. Let them use pictures to communicate and convey their thoughts.

If your child has a favourite story that is read every day:

2. When you reach certain parts of a story, recite partially and encourage your child to complete it.
3. Ask them, "Can you remember what happens next?"
4. Let them visualise and 'fill in the blanks.'
5. Add small mistakes or skip some parts of the story. Is your child able to detect them?

For older children:

1. Guide them in keeping a dream journal or a diary to stimulate visualisation abilities.
2. Put up a project board or picture board in a central area of your home for brainstorming of ideas.

2. VISUALISATION GAMES

Why:

Most children display an interest in art. It is particularly beneficial for visualisation games. This is not just to make learning visible; it is also an outlet for your child to express themselves. Visuals make it easier and quicker for them to grasp the meaning of complex concepts.

Imagination is the ability to produce mental images in one's mind. However, it is often misguided, particularly in Asian society with its result-based education system.

Regrettably, this is regarded as whimsical and trivial. Evidence shows that observers and daydreamers are often the most thoughtful and have abilities to 'visualise' difficult abstract concepts. Parents can encourage it and take actions to direct this skill.

3. LOGICAL REASONING GAMES

- Your child can make rational sense of information that is collected.
- Often, some children repeatedly ask their parents 'Why?' because they are trying to reason and rationalise.

Beyond Grades

Steps:
1. Encourage curiosity.
2. When your child asks 'Why?'
3. Turn the question around and respond, 'What do you think?'
4. Follow-up and respond.
5. If they do not reply, do not be critical. Encourage them.
6. You can also turn it into a 'Why?' game.

Example:
If it is raining and they cannot go to the playground now. Ask them why they should not be outdoors and maintain this line of questioning—because it is raining; because they have no raincoat; because they will fall sick.

Why:
This activity will stretch their logical reasoning and train them to think in cause – effect or action – consequence. This technique can also be used to encourage older children to think about forward-thinking concepts and also a skill that is necessary for advanced level exam questions.

3. LOGICAL REASONING GAMES

Asian culture often represses the natural quality of children to collect information, discouraging them from repeatedly asking why – a harmful culture. Our children are often encouraged to not question further about any information they receive just out of curiosity. This traditional, hierarchical belief that youngsters are not allowed to 'challenge' their elders (or parents) is harmful to the child.

Your child's inquisitiveness should never be ignored because it shows that your child is attempting to reason and rationalise. If you ignore them, you are teaching the child that silence or abstinence is the answer. Your child will think that doing nothing is the correct way to rationalise and reason a concept.

4. MEMORY GAMES	
• How does your child store and retrieve information to make sense of the world? • Your child needs to pay attention to the world around them.	**Fun with Memory** **Steps:** 1. Let your child be involved in daily activities 2. Let them pack their own school bag. 3. Start with a mini treasure hunt to collect particular items and place them in the bag. 4. While on the journey to school in the car, ask your child to recall what they helped you pack. 5. If they forgot, give them hints to let them figure out themselves—what colour, where was it found, what it is used for. Do the same for other daily co-curricular activities 1. Play the tray game, a classic memory game perfect for all ages and children in groups. 2. Put items on a tray and ask the child to remember them. 3. Place some objects on a tray in no particular order. A variety of shapes and sizes work best. **Why:** When they do something or speak, it is output from their brain, which completes the loop of their brain-based process: Input-Process-Output, thus enhancing memory and understanding.

5. PROCESSING SPEED GAMES

- How fast your child gives meaning to the collected information.
- A child slow in processing info or instructions risk being left behind, particularly in school.
- Therefore, as parents, it is crucial to help your children improve their cognitive processing speed at home.

The Speed Factor

Steps:
1. Get an identical or similar puzzle and race against your child to see who can complete the puzzle first.
2. Give them an achievable goal so they will be motivated to improve.
3. Pace yourself, so you match the pace of your child. You can win first (by a small margin), but you should also give your child a taste of success to motivate them.
4. Eventually, your child should be allowed to win and with much praise.
5. You can speed up the game as your child's processing speed improves.
6. Older children can engage in processing speed with structured games like chess or checkers.

Why:
Keep the atmosphere of competition balanced and avoid over-competitiveness.

Summary

Everyone is a Winner

Guided play will help children explore, discover, take risks, create meaning and solve problems based on their natural motivations. Such simple play-based activities will help stretch and strengthen your child's cognitive muscles, often without the child even realising it.

For all the mental games described in this chapter, you should applaud successes while gently addressing failures.

THE 5 MENTAL GAMES TO HELP YOUR CHILD'S MENTAL ABILITIES

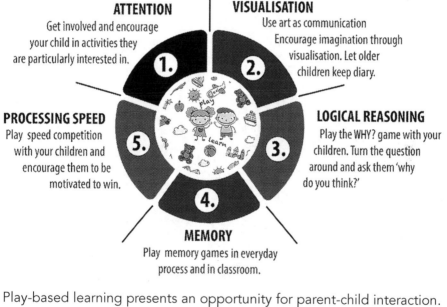

ATTENTION
Get involved and encourage your child in activities they are particularly interested in.

VISUALISATION
Use art as communication
Encourage imagination through visualisation. Let older children keep diary.

PROCESSING SPEED
Play speed competition with your children and encourage them to be motivated to win.

LOGICAL REASONING
Play the WHY? game with your children. Turn the question around and ask them 'why do you think?'

MEMORY
Play memory games in everyday process and in classroom.

Play-based learning presents an opportunity for parent-child interaction. Parents can engage with their child in the dual role of a parent and a trusted guide. It is well-documented that parents who become a trusted friend and respected guide have successful parent-child relationships, which contributes to personality development and successful learning [v].

Parents play the most crucial role as you spend the most time with your child at home. Just make it a habit during your daily routines and activities, be it in the car or when having meals, **actively communicate** to stimulate your child's thinking. Make it a part of your daily life and have fun!

CHAPTER 5

BrainThink Learning

Introduction

In Chapter 3: 5 Brain Abilities, we explore how the brain works and how we can effectively facilitate our child's learning to get the best results. To briefly recap—the brain of a young child is flexible and easily adaptable to conditioning; which is why the way we educate our child is critical to how our child's brain develops.

Ever-expanding research indicates brain-based learning is the optimal approach to promote the five brain abilities—Attention, Visualisation, Memory, Logic Reasoning and Processing Speed.

What can you learn from this chapter?

This chapter will elaborate on how BrainThink Learning achieves the building of your child's cognitive skills.

You will learn about:

- What are BrainThink Learning and its components
- The three success factors and the five-stage process of BrainThink Learning
- How BrainThink Learning is based on 2 heavily researched principles
- What is meaningful learning and the 12 Principles of Natural Learning
- The importance of variety in learning
- What is Active Learning

A Holistic Approach to Meaningful Learning

BrainThink Learning stems from the methodologies of brain-based learning, a form of holistic education. This approach targets the learner's personality, emotions, physical needs, and the surrounding environment while promoting the processes of cognitive skills.

Here are general differences between conventional learning and holistic approach to meaningful education:

Here are several popular brain-based learning methodologies.

Conventional Learning	Brain-based Learning

• Syllabi-driven • Memory intensive • Focus on grades and exams	• Open and natural minded • Flexible • Tailored to capabilities

Meaningful Learning is in Context, Experiential and Tailored

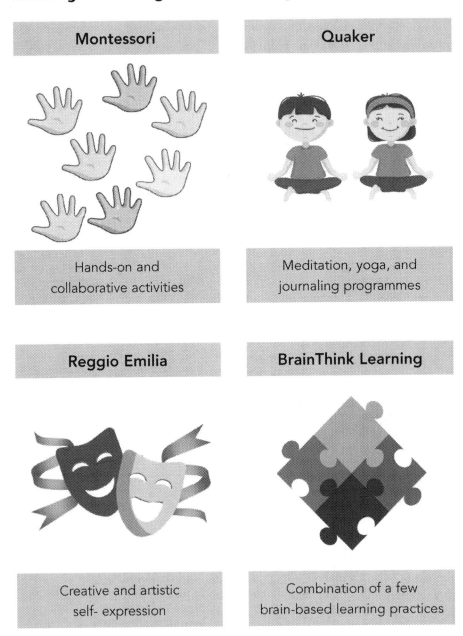

Montessori	Quaker
Hands-on and collaborative activities	Meditation, yoga, and journaling programmes
Reggio Emilia	BrainThink Learning
Creative and artistic self- expression	Combination of a few brain-based learning practices

Meaningful Learning is in Context, Experiential and Tailored

BrainThink applies the 12 Natural Learning Principles as set forth by Caine & Caine, leading brain-based learning researchers.

12 Natural Learning Principles

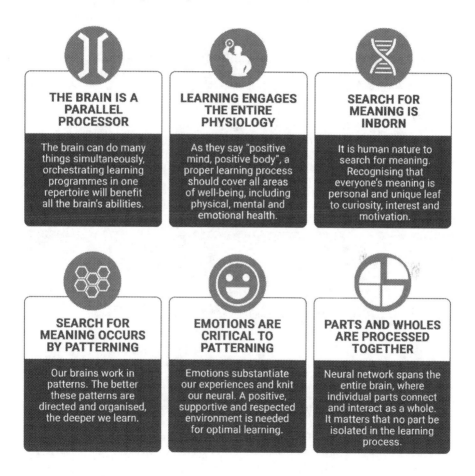

THE BRAIN IS A PARALLEL PROCESSOR

The brain can do many things simultaneously, orchestrating learning programmes in one repertoire will benefit all the brain's abilities.

LEARNING ENGAGES THE ENTIRE PHYSIOLOGY

As they say "positive mind, positive body", a proper learning process should cover all areas of well-being, including physical, mental and emotional health.

SEARCH FOR MEANING IS INBORN

It is human nature to search for meaning. Recognising that everyone's meaning is personal and unique leaf to curiosity, interest and motivation.

SEARCH FOR MEANING OCCURS BY PATTERNING

Our brains work in patterns. The better these patterns are directed and organised, the deeper we learn.

EMOTIONS ARE CRITICAL TO PATTERNING

Emotions substantiate our experiences and knit our neural. A positive, supportive and respected environment is needed for optimal learning.

PARTS AND WHOLES ARE PROCESSED TOGETHER

Neural network spans the entire brain, where individual parts connect and interact as a whole. It matters that no part be isolated in the learning process.

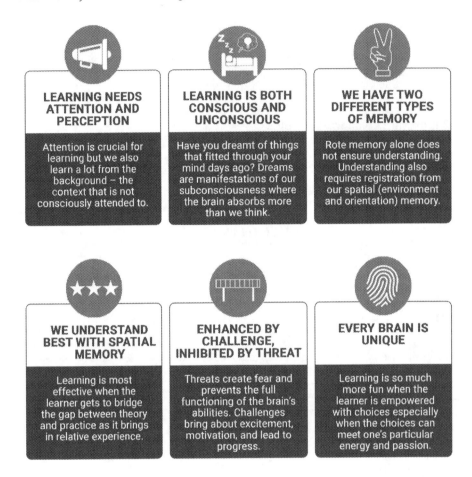

LEARNING NEEDS ATTENTION AND PERCEPTION

Attention is crucial for learning but we also learn a lot from the background – the context that is not consciously attended to.

LEARNING IS BOTH CONSCIOUS AND UNCONSCIOUS

Have you dreamt of things that fitted through your mind days ago? Dreams are manifestations of our subconsciousness where the brain absorbs more than we think.

WE HAVE TWO DIFFERENT TYPES OF MEMORY

Rote memory alone does not ensure understanding. Understanding also requires registration from our spatial (environment and orientation) memory.

WE UNDERSTAND BEST WITH SPATIAL MEMORY

Learning is most effective when the learner gets to bridge the gap between theory and practice as it brings in relative experience.

ENHANCED BY CHALLENGE, INHIBITED BY THREAT

Threats create fear and prevents the full functioning of the brain's abilities. Challenges bring about excitement, motivation, and lead to progress.

EVERY BRAIN IS UNIQUE

Learning is so much more fun when the learner is empowered with choices especially when the choices can meet one's particular energy and passion.

In short, learning is meaningful when it is in context, experiential, and tailored. We learn faster and better when we can resonate with the subject matter. Familiarity enables the brain to build consistent patterns with existing knowledge, which in turn enhances the overall learning process. The experience should be personal and relative, i.e. adapted to the learner's context or level.

However, how does BrainThink Learning address these principles in practice?

Curiosity - Explore - Test - Repeat - Master

BrainThink Learning's **Curiosity-Explore-Test-Repeat-Master** is a 5-stage process that takes the 5 brain abilities through its natural **Input-Process-Output** development methodically, logically, and comprehensively.

Each stage correlates the principles of brain-based learning supplemented by the activation of all 5 brain abilities through a variety of creative and well-planned teaching methods. The diagram below illustrates how every stage leads to your child's mastery of learning.

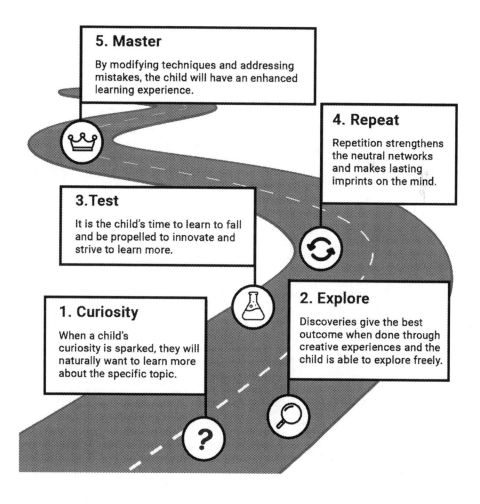

5. Master

By modifying techniques and addressing mistakes, the child will have an enhanced learning experience.

4. Repeat

Repetition strengthens the neutral networks and makes lasting imprints on the mind.

3. Test

It is the child's time to learn to fall and be propelled to innovate and strive to learn more.

1. Curiosity

When a child's curiosity is sparked, they will naturally want to learn more about the specific topic.

2. Explore

Discoveries give the best outcome when done through creative experiences and the child is able to explore freely.

Variety is the Spice of Learning

BrainThink Learning draws its strengths from two majorly researched premises to power its approach.

1. Cone of Learning

Edgar Dale, a distinguished American educator, theorized that learners retain more information by what they "do" as opposed to what was "heard", "read" or "saw". His Cone of Experience lists the hierarchical effectiveness of a range of stimuli on the brain.

Cone of Learning provides learning models that allow educators to understand how to increase the retention rate of learners by involving the learner. This means when the children participate and get involved in the learning process by doing, they awaken the sensory organs to increase the retention.

"I see and I forget, I hear and I remember, I do and I understand."

—Confucius

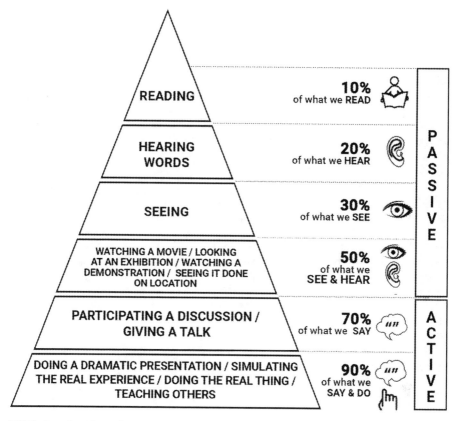

With further involvement, we tend to remember and understand the subject better.

With **BrainThink Learning**, children shall be guided to explore and discover information instead of direct instruction. Then, through the **Play to Learn** approach, educators facilitate the children to apply their knowledge in a fun setting or play environment. Children are encouraged to teach their friends, which will help confirm their understanding. Active learning methods increase overall learning effectiveness. Let's shift from merely memorising information to meaningful learning.

2. Bloom's Taxonomy

Bloom's Taxonomy is a framework used by educators to classify learning objectives based on complexity and specificity. The taxonomy allows educators to design performance tasks, craft questions and provide feedback to students. It gives them ways to think about their educational processes and the subsequent learning of their students.

According to the revised Bloom's Taxonomy in 2001, "REMEMBER" information is the lowest skillset to achieve while "CREATE" new ideas or products from information are the highest skillset and most difficult to master. The Taxonomy lists out the cognitive processes involved under each category, a useful guide to refer to during lesson planning and delivery.

CREATE
Produce New or Original Work
Design, assemble, construct, conjecture, develop, formulate, author, investigate

EVALUATE
Justify A Stand or Decision
Appraise, argue, defend, judge, select, supports, value, critique, weigh

ANALYSE
Draw Connections Among Ideas
Differentiate, organise, relate compare, contrast, distinguish, examine, experiment, test

APPLY
Use information in new situation
Execute, implement, solve, use, demonstrate, interpret, operate, schedule, sketch

UNDERSTAND
Explain ideas or concepts
Classify, describe, discuss, explain, identity, locate, organise, report, select translate

REMEMBER
Recall Facts and basic concepts
Define, duplicate, list, memorise, repeat, state translate

Would your child grow up with a 360-degree perspective?

Have you heard of the tale about **The Blind Men and the Elephant?** The blind men could only relate to the one perception (touch) they had, and though they were all correct in their judgments, they were still unable to agree on what the elephant looked like.

This tale points out that the views of our world can be biased if we are not fully informed, lack general objectivity and open-mindedness. To be able to see **the big picture,** we must be armed with all our perceptions, a 360-degree view.

We must experience a variety of stimuli to strengthen our 5 brain abilities and to form a better view of our world. That is why Dale's Cone of Experience and Bloom's Taxonomy are at the forefront of **BrainThink Learning.**

The Success Factors—Play. Think. Learn.

√ BrainThink practises brain-based learning within the framework of **Play. Think. Learn.**

√ We know that children love to play, and this play is essential to raise curiosity and facilitate their learning.

√ Games make powerful learning tools when devised to fit a learning objective and implemented with all the principles mentioned above.

√ Lessons that make learning through play are valued commodities.

What Play Does to Cognitive Skills

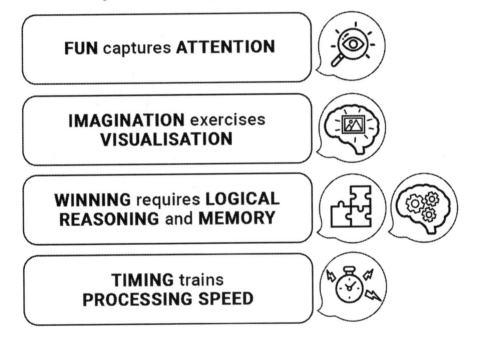

FUN captures **ATTENTION**

IMAGINATION exercises **VISUALISATION**

WINNING requires **LOGICAL REASONING** and **MEMORY**

TIMING trains **PROCESSING SPEED**

Summary

Getting Your Child's Brain to Think with the Soul

Cognitive lessons awaken the "soul" of your child's mind, and BrainThink is an engineer of such learnings.

BrainThink Learning is a brain-based methodology that stimulates children's brain to think cognitively, rather than by rote. It aims to produce whole-rounded individuals who are positive and confident; able to tackle problems and approach life without fear.

Putting BrainThink into perspective, here is a simplified diagram to illustrate the two comprising components of BrainThink Learning.

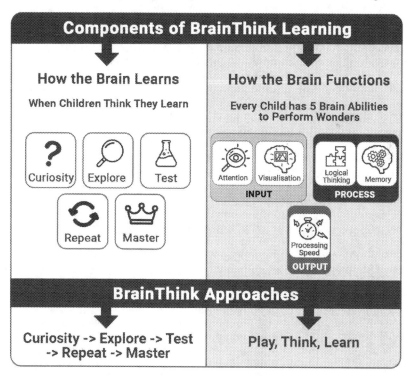

BrainThink Learning will strengthen your child's 5 brain abilities and problem solving capability with integrating the concepts of Bloom's Taxanomy and Dale's Cone of Learning, which apply these two approaches: **Curiosity-Explore-Test-Repeat-Master** and **Play-Think-Learn.**

CHAPTER 6

Why Should I Foster Creative Learning in My Child?

Introduction

"We especially need imagination in science. It is not all mathematics, nor all logic, but it is somewhat beauty and poetry."

—Maria Mitchell

Creativity is vital to promote the healthy intellectual, social, and emotional development of your child. It is a critical element of effective learning and should be inculcated as early as possible to ensure your child becomes a well-rounded and highly capable person.

The traditional, naïve view that creativity is for a child who is not excelling academically is dated, old-fashioned and uninformed. Everyone can be creative! Just as how children are not equally intelligent, they are not creative in the same way as well. This explains why it is not uncommon that many parents assume that creativity is something that their children either do or do not have.

However, that is not the case. As you read on, you will discover that creative abilities can be developed, and you have a role in fostering creative learning in your children. As parents, you can help your children in the development of their creative skills by first equipping yourself with the knowledge and skills to practice with your children at home.

What can you learn from this chapter?

This chapter talks about every child's ability to be creative, the importance of developing their creative skills and teaching parents on how they can nurture creativity in their own homes.

The topics we will cover include:

- Children's Creative Abilities Come in All Forms and Levels
- How You Can Nurture Creativity at Home

Children's Creative Abilities Come in All Forms and Levels

People have assumptions about creativity, but these are the facts:

✗ Fiction	✓ Fact
• Creativity is a talent that some children have while others do not. • Creativity is only for children who are not excelling academically. • Creativity purely involves artistic and musical expression.	• Creativity is not inborn. Rather, it is a skill that parents can help their child to develop. • Creativity is vital for all children because it is a key component in their intellectual development. • Creativity is necessary for Science and Mathematics too.

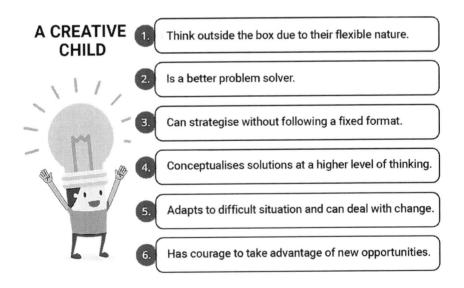

A CREATIVE CHILD

1. Think outside the box due to their flexible nature.
2. Is a better problem solver.
3. Can strategise without following a fixed format.
4. Conceptualises solutions at a higher level of thinking.
5. Adapts to difficult situation and can deal with change.
6. Has courage to take advantage of new opportunities.

Creativity is recognised as one of the core elements of learning effectively. Therefore, it is equally important to practice and nurture this core skill in your children.

How You Can Nurture Creativity at Home

Recent research found that it was the style of parenting, rather than the parents' income that developed the strength of character and intellect in a child.

Following this, there are reliable, research-based, educational activities that can foster an effective and creative learning style within your child.

1. TIME AND SPACE

Steps:
1. Encourage children to read for pleasure, not just for studying.
2. Limit TV and other screen time to make room for creative activities.

For younger children
1. Activities should be child-directed and not influenced by adult interference.
2. Allocate a specific place where your child can make a mess.
3. Get them art supplies or building materials as gifts or birthday presents.
4. Put them in storage boxes where your child can access at any time.

Why:
A 'dress-up box' or a 'props box' encourages your child to use 'Visualisation' while a 'building box' or 'art box' involves 'Logical Reasoning'.

1. TIME AND SPACE

For older children
1. Teach them to use their time for more mature activities like journal writing.

Why:
Besides improved creative writing and literacy skills, journal writing will engage their 'Attention' and 'Logical Reasoning' abilities. They will learn to search for successful answers through careful reflection and evaluation.

2. ATMOSPHERE

Steps:
1. Expand their cultural knowledge by exploring art exhibitions and galleries.
2. Play classical or tasteful music softly at home to give a cultural ambience.
3. Line the walls of your home with art that you like.
4. Tell your child why you like a specific painting or book and show an interest in architecture or photography.

Why:
To turn your home into space for creativity, you need to foster a creative atmosphere. Celebrating your own innovation and creativity helps develop strength in character and creative intellect in your child.

3. CREATIVE ATTITUDE

Embrace Failure

Steps:
1. Develop a Growth Mindset: Encourage your child to make mistakes and fail.
2. Share the mistakes you've made in a light-hearted way and laugh about how many great people have had significant failures before they succeeded.

Example:
Tell your child stories like how 12 publishers rejected J.K. Rowling's first Harry Potter book before eventually being considered.

Why:
Such stories help your child to understand that making mistakes is normal and what is important is to learn to recover from them to achieve ultimate success. These prevent them from restricting their creative thought through a 'fear of failure' mental conditioning.

Have a Neutral Attitude

Steps:
1. Resist the urge to evaluate or judge the ideas your child suggests.
2. Listen to what your child has in mind or prompt them with some possible suggestions on what could be done.
3. Be encouraging with their creative ideas as this will stretch their imagination further and lead to an open-minded attitude.

Example:
During brainstorming activities, encourage your child to think of things they have never done before. Be careful not to decide which ideas are the best or not possible — stay neutral.

Why:
Neutrality shows that you consider and respect their view. The aim is to expand their thinking process, i.e. generating versus evaluating new ideas.

4. DIVERGENT THOUGHTS

Steps:
1. Prompt your child to find more than one route to a solution, and more than one answer to a problem.
2. Allow your child the freedom and autonomy to explore ideas.
3. Keep in mind that what may seem like a ridiculous idea is also a 'think-out-of-the-box' idea.
4. Encourage older children to participate in drama classes and clubs where they can freely express themselves.

Example:
Prompt your child to find another route to school by car or a way to make the same LEGO 'character' without following the set instructions.

Why:
Thinking in different directions is an essential skill for solving problems.

5. TOUGH LOVE

Steps:
1. Tough love is not about caning your child, which is negative and not progressive.
2. Do not reward children for simply exhibiting creativity.
3. Allow children to develop mastery of creative activities that they are naturally motivated to do, rather than trying to drive them with constant rewards and incentives.

Why:
Research supports the fact that parents who use a mixture of discipline and warmth are most likely to produce well-rounded individuals who succeed in all areas of life, with creativity as a central skill in the journey. It builds up a child's self-esteem but also teaches them to be restrained and respectful.

Summary

How You Can Nurture Creativity at Home

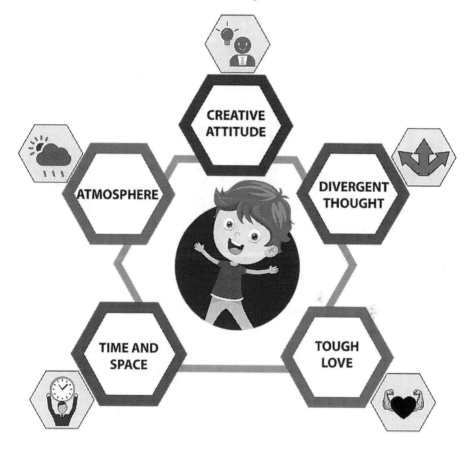

In conclusion, by following these steps or approaches, neither are you allowing your child to do what they want nor encouraging them to be 'non-academic'— precisely the opposite, in fact, which is a good thing.

You are guiding and developing their freedom of thought and flexing the muscles in their brain. Alongside the expertise provided by methodologies such as BrainThink Learning and programmes such as MathBrain, you are contributing to your child's role in society as a whole and their prosperous intellectual future.

CHAPTER 7

MathBrain For Your Child

Introduction

"Math is like going to the gym for your brain. It sharpens your mind."
—Danica McKellar

Are you curious about **MathBrain** and what it is all about? To shed some light on the matter, we will need to revisit the red and white balls exercise from Chapter 3.

> **We have red balls in 1 basket and white balls in another basket. We want to find out how many red balls and white balls there are. 2 equations:**
> 1) If we take 1 red ball and 1 white ball out from the baskets each time, eventually, red ball basket will be empty, and there are 50 white balls left in the other basket.
> 2) If we take 1 red ball and 3 white balls out from the baskets each time, eventually, white ball basket will be empty, and there are 50 red balls left in the other basket.

Points to ponder about:
1) Can you figure out the number of red and white balls? (Do not use algebra as this is meant for primary school children).
2) Is this a math question?
3) Can you use your memory or any formula to find the answer to this question?
4) What brain abilities are needed to solve this question?

5) How many times did your brain "process" to:
- Gather accurate information?
- Understand the relationship between the numbers in the equations?
- Try to figure out various ways to find the answer?
- Try to apply appropriate formulae to find the answer?

6) Did your brain:
- "**Explore** possible ways to find the answer?"
- "**Test** if the possible answer is correct?" and
- "**Repeat** with the possible ways and **Test** it again to see if you can find the answer?"

MathBrain abilities would be in position to be confident to process and solve such a question as shown above.

However, Math is a unique thing. You can also arrive at the same conclusion with different solving paths. Here's are some examples:

The Math Problem:

23 x 11 = ?

Method 1: Conventional (taught in schools)

```
        2  3
  x     1  1
  ----------
        2  3
  +  2  3  0
  ----------
     2  5  3
```

Method 2: Vertical and Crosswise (One of Vedic Sutra)

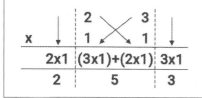

Method 3: Magic of 11 - Add the Neighbour ("zero" when nothing at the side).

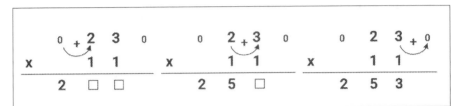

Points to Ponder:

1) Do you think the above methods are confusing? Or is your brain confused?

2) Compare the other methods with Method 1, which method is the fastest to find the answer?

3) Are the methods using the same or different principles?

4) Can you accept these methods?

5) These methods have no conflicts. Anyone with **MathBrain** ability can see the exact calculation similarities from a different angle.

   5.1 Method 2 is another angle of method 1

   5.2 Method 3 is also different angle of method 1. In method 1, you can see that nothing ('0') was added to 2, 2 add to 3, 3 add to nothing ('0').

**Can you see that these 3 methods
are using the same principles?**

**Try to see from different angles and
you can find they are similar.**

What can you learn from this chapter?

Find out what MathBrain is all about as we cover the following:

- The importance of Mathematics in our lives
- Why you should equip yourself with the ever powerful and indispensable tool—Math
- How to shift your learning from procedural to conceptual
- Grow your child with MathBrain
- Play: the winning formula
- BrainThink Learning paves the way for MathBrain
- The best education for our children

The Importance of Mathematics

"Mathematics possesses not only truth but supreme beauty."
—Bertrand Russell

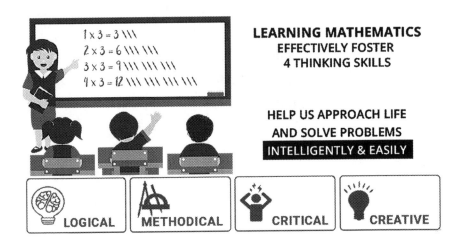

Applications of Mathematics in our daily life are inevitable. Thus, learning Math is essential.

- **On a shopping trip:** addition, subtraction and estimation
- **When staying fit and healthy:** the balancing of calorie-counts with body fat percentage and mass index
- **Improve homes & save costs:** trigonometric calculations for wall structures, pipe installations and light angles
- **Plan financial budgets & investments:** algebraic understanding of exponential growth
- Science, Technology, Geography, Music and many more disciplines use Mathematics too

Moving Learning from Procedural to Conceptual

Anyone can have the MathBrain ability, with the proper guidance and training in an excellent curriculum. We believe that holistic BrainThink Learning, a type of brain-based learning, is the best route to helping develop their MathBrain. BrainThink Learning approach has effects on the improvement of students' motivation and achievement in learning Mathematics [vi].

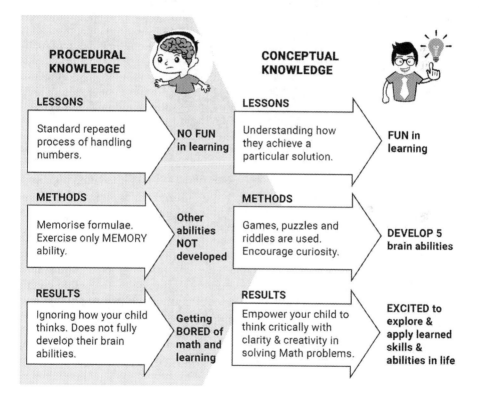

PROCEDURAL KNOWLEDGE		CONCEPTUAL KNOWLEDGE	
LESSONS Standard repeated process of handling numbers.	**NO FUN in learning**	**LESSONS** Understanding how they achieve a particular solution.	**FUN in learning**
METHODS Memorise formulae. Exercise only MEMORY ability.	**Other abilities NOT developed**	**METHODS** Games, puzzles and riddles are used. Encourage curiosity.	**DEVELOP 5 brain abilities**
RESULTS Ignoring how your child thinks. Does not fully develop their brain abilities.	**Getting BORED of math and learning**	**RESULTS** Empower your child to think critically with clarity & creativity in solving Math problems.	**EXCITED to explore & apply learned skills & abilities in life**

What is MathBrain?

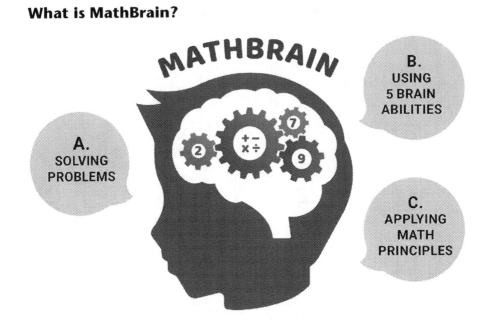

MathBrain is the **ability to solve problems** using the **5 brain abilities** with **math principles**. With MathBrain, a child would be able to explore their 5 brain abilities in applying math principles to solve problems.

A child would be able to:

- gather accurate information from a math problem (**Attention**),
- understand the meaningful relationship between numerical symbols and words (**Visualisation**),
- figure out the different ways of solving the problem (**Logical Thinking**),
- apply appropriate methods or formulae to solve the problem (**Memory**), and
- derive the answer quickly and accurately (**Processing Speed**).

Grow Your Child with MathBrain

By making mathematics fun, children will not only enjoy themselves, but they will also be skilled with numbers and numerical symbols. Make it easy with simple mathematical problems and their mind will be open to doing more while they have fun. Their excitement will grow their mind to think naturally. They will go through the BrainThink learning process of **Curiosities-Explore-Test-Repeat-Master** as their mind undergoes **Input-Process-Output** with their **5 Brain Abilities.**

Building the 5 Brain Abilities	Into the Learning of Mathematics
1. ATTENTION	

- Your child's brain can be trained to focus for long periods of time and to withstand distractions.
- You don't need to ask your child to "Pay Attention!"
- If the lesson appeals to their curiosity, their attention will be engaged.
- When attention is present, implicit learning (learning of complex information in an incidental manner) takes place automatically, and content is more readily absorbed.
- Regular practice improves resistance to distractions.

» A simple game-like lesson can bring out your child's sense of fun and direct their attention.
» Increasing the game's 'levels' through strategic win-and-achieve completion leads to motivation.
» Repeatedly done in a variety of ways nicely works to train habits of constant focus.

Sample activity: Challenge your child to order a series of digits into a given numerical sequence.

Building the 5 Brain Abilities	Into the Learning of Mathematics
2. VISUALISATION	

- Visualisation helps to break down the task of interpreting text and figures, which can sometimes be too intensive to read through, or, for the early learners, too unfamiliar a subject.
- This breakdown makes it easier for your child's brain to assimilate the content.
- Three questions matter:
  - o What is in the picture?
  - o What do you see that makes you say that?
  - o What more can we find?

» Mathematics is the interweaving of patterns. Encourage children to visualise mathematical questions as clear patterns reduce the focus on the 'problem' and build confidence in deriving solutions.

» Expressing these questions in games also teaches the children the meaningful connections between rules and outcomes.

Sample activity: Task your child to illustrate a worded mathematical problem graphically.

Building the 5 Brain Abilities	Into the Learning of Mathematics

3. LOGICAL REASONING

- This skill is dependent on your child's cognitive abilities working together to integrate all the information their brain has stored to conclude. The more information stored, the better equipped your child is to make wholesome deductions.
- Building a comprehensive 'store' can only be achieved when your child's brain has had the chance to capture information in a variety of postures and from a range of reality-based experiences.

» An effective curriculum should include both concrete and abstract instructions so that your child receives full exposure to gather knowledge.

» These games or activities should also demonstrate the relations between rules and mathematical operations. Understanding them will enable your child to form numerical mental patterns to better 'see' the information towards making conclusions.

Sample activity: Set a patterned activity, where your child needs to observe its trend and fill in the blanks.

Building the 5 Brain Abilities	Into the Learning of Mathematics
4. MEMORY	

- We have three kinds of memory, each dependent on the next for full understanding.
- Activating attention leads to the first, 'short-term memory'.
- Continual engagement and motivation of the first, enable the information retained to move into the second, 'working memory'. This is when your child assesses the information and gains understanding of the process.
- Repetition in the second phase cements the knowledge acquired, bringing it into the third, 'long-term memory'.

» The best way to take the boredom out of any memorising exercise is to turn it into something fun.
» With indulgence and immersion in such activities, your child would not even realise that they are memorising the information!
» The objective is to promote faster memory retention for quick recall and good processing ability.

Sample activity: Time your child to all-time-favourite memory games involving symbols and numbers.

Building the 5 Brain Abilities	Into the Learning of Mathematics
5. PROCESSING SPEED	

• This has nothing to do with intelligence. It is merely a fact that strong and broad cognitive abilities enable your child's brain to 'connect' its neural networks faster, allowing them to grasp concepts easier and quicker. • It results in efficient brain processing and helps your child tackle tasks much smoother.	» Adding competitive and timed elements to game-based activities in lessons can increase your child's processing speed. » Training should start with information in smaller chunks, building up in intensity as their brain develops and is ready for more.

Sample activity: Devise a mathematical crossword puzzle based on an exciting theme relevant to your child.

Play—The Winning Formula

Play is essential to the health of your child's brain. It naturally triggers hormones in our bodies that stimulate the growth of brain cells and those that make us feel good [vii].

The pleasure of having free imagination while at play will help your child to relax and de-stress—the same 'easy' environment prescribed for effective BrainThink learning.

Children with healthy brain abilities can comprehend easier and faster, resulting in confidence that expands their curiosity and interest for more knowledge.

Play. Think. Learn. is the backbone of **BrainThink Learning** for children.

Makes *play* synonymous with learning.

1

Easily integrates your support (as an adult/educator) where you play & guide your child simultaneously.

2

The 'Play. Think. Learn.' Approach

Allows parents/teachers the flexibility of applying various methods and styles to meet the child's learning abilities & objectives.

3

4

Gives your child the freedom to create through experience, to self-learn from their own choices.

BrainThink Paves the Way for MathBrain

BrainThink Learning delivery concentrates on fun activities to improve your child's capabilities to be motivated to learn.

Vedic Mathematics principles are used as math principles; a simple, fast, and intuitive approach. Removing the rigidity in 'conventional' methods, it truly complements the fun theme in BrainThink learning!

Vedic Math

Circa early 1900, Indian scholar, Bharati Krishna Tirthaji, theorised that we could work out any mathematical problem using a suite of powerful 16 formulae (he called them Vedic Sutras) in one coherent technique [viii] :

√ Sutras work in patterns like those in our brain, 'vertically and diagonally'.
√ No approach is wrong as the Sutras are flexible and can be creatively manipulated to arrive at the same answer.
√ Solutions involve only a few steps and do not require calculators.
√ The methodology's simplicity means that one can do it mentally, making it efficient and fast.
√ It cultivates mental agility, thereby meeting the brain-based learning's criteria to improve all the 5 brain abilities.

Refer to the diagrams on the next page for some Vedic Math's tricks:

Example 1: Division

$$294 \div 3 = 3 \quad | \quad 2_2\,9_2\,4$$

$$098$$

Steps:

1) $2 \div 3 = 0$ remainder 2. Write the 2 next to the following digit, 9, making it 29.

2) $29 \div 3 = 9$ remainder 2. Write the 2 next to the following digit, 4, making it 24.

3) $24 \div 3 = 8$.

4) The answer is 98.

Example 2: Subtraction

$$1000 - 357 = ?$$

Steps:

We simply take each figure in 357 from 9 and the last value from 10.

1) $9 - 3 = 6$

2) $9 - 5 = 4$

3) $10 - 7 = 3$

4) Therefore, $1000 - 357 = 643$.

Summary

The Best Education for Our Children

"Children must be taught how to think, not what to think"

—Margaret Mead

The best education for our children needs to be interactive and experiential. We should not strive to make our children more 'intelligent'; instead, we should aim to make them wise and well rounded, cognitively equipped to be future-ready while building their intelligence.

The Best Education for Our Children

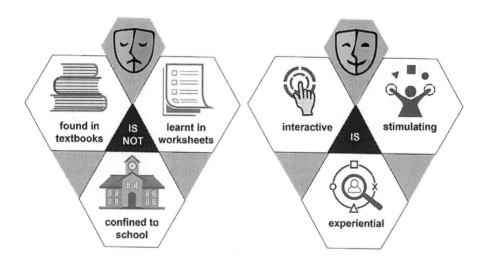

CHAPTER 8

Discover Your Child's 5 Brain Abilities

Introduction

"Education is not the learning of facts,
   but the training of the mind to think."

—Albert Einstein

The brain is one of the most integral parts of our bodies. It controls the way we think and behave. Its capabilities dictate our entire being. Its development shapes all our actions. Understanding its makeup and nature will lead us to make it work smartly.

Unfortunately, the most common learning methods used today by educators tend to develop only our memory skills. Optimising our brainpower is more than just memory; we need to be able to fully utilise and maximise our brain's 5 major abilities—attention, visualisation, logical thinking, memory and processing speed.

As parents, you need to know your child's brain capacity and capabilities. Now, why is that so important? This is so that you'll learn to create a conducive environment at home for your children. Moreover, children today are learning at a faster speed and absorbing more information than we can keep up. That is why you'll be a smart and well-informed parent in identifying appropriate learning programmes that fit your child's development.

This chapter aims to demonstrate how the brain works so that we can take the appropriate actions to help it perform optimally. You'll also discover the importance of assessing your child's brain abilities and decide what you should do next.

What can you learn from this chapter?

- Learn about the brain and its abilities
- Discover why the brain's Input-Process-Output (IPO) matters
- Why as parents, you need to understand your child's 5 Brain Abilities
- The 5 Brain Abilities Assessment and how to get the assessment for your child

The Brain and Its Abilities

The brain's physical architecture

There is a common misconception about our brain's build and physical structure.

Common belief	Latest scientific research suggests
• The brain develops only during gestation • It builds within a blueprint • The architecture is shaped by our genes and is fixed	• Our brain is malleable and adaptable • It is subject to its environment as we grow

How the brain works

Here's a simplified explanation of how our brain forms its architecture—how we learn something and become good at it.

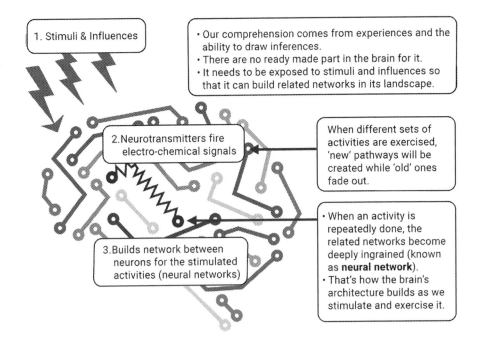

1. Stimuli & Influences

• Our comprehension comes from experiences and the ability to draw inferences.
• There are no ready made part in the brain for it.
• It needs to be exposed to stimuli and influences so that it can build related networks in its landscape.

2. Neurotransmitters fire electro-chemical signals

When different sets of activities are exercised, 'new' pathways will be created while 'old' ones fade out.

3. Builds network between neurons for the stimulated activities (neural networks)

• When an activity is repeatedly done, the related networks become deeply ingrained (known as **neural network**).
• That's how the brain's architecture builds as we stimulate and exercise it.

Points to ponder

- Neuroscientists found that blind people who read Braille with their fingers have larger sensory cortices.
- In another research, they found that people who learn languages from images and sounds possess higher reading proficiency than those who learn just from alphabets. The group that learned from alphabets strictly, without images or visuals tended to use the right brain (right occipitotemporal cortex), which, incidentally, is the area linked with reading difficulties.

Our children's brain is one flexible muscle

- The younger the brain, the more flexible and adjustable to conditioning.
- Various types and quality of stimuli with different levels of influences will shape our children's brain architecture.
- Play to Learn or any education will have crucial influence that can change the construction of the brain.
- Mutually, the expanse and shape of its architecture also affect our children's ability to learn.

The Brain's Cognitive Abilities

Let us look into how the physical brain performs and process.

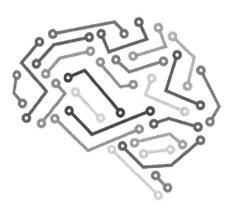

- The neural networks in our brain determine our cognitive abilities (i.e. brain abilities).
- The more developed the networks, the better the brain performs.
- As mentioned in Chapter 3, when learning takes place, the connections (or synapses) in a child's brain become stronger and permanent while unstimulated synapses die off.
- As such, we can safely say that the stronger the skills of your child, the more cognitive they become.

Our brain abilities are essential core skills for us to function daily.

Think   **Act**   **Engage**

The 5 major brain abilities

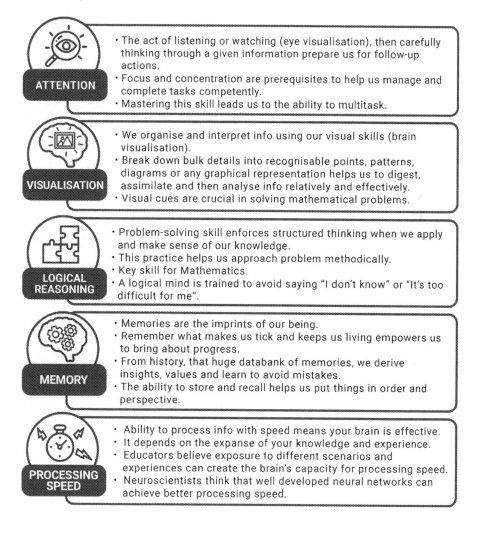

ATTENTION
- The act of listening or watching (eye visualisation), then carefully thinking through a given information prepare us for follow-up actions.
- Focus and concentration are prerequisites to help us manage and complete tasks competently.
- Mastering this skill leads us to the ability to multitask.

VISUALISATION
- We organise and interpret info using our visual skills (brain visualisation).
- Break down bulk details into recognisable points, patterns, diagrams or any graphical representation helps us to digest, assimilate and then analyse info relatively and effectively.
- Visual cues are crucial in solving mathematical problems.

LOGICAL REASONING
- Problem-solving skill enforces structured thinking when we apply and make sense of our knowledge.
- This practice helps us approach problem methodically.
- Key skill for Mathematics.
- A logical mind is trained to avoid saying "I don't know" or "It's too difficult for me".

MEMORY
- Memories are the imprints of our being.
- Remember what makes us tick and keeps us living empowers us to bring about progress.
- From history, that huge databank of memories, we derive insights, values and learn to avoid mistakes.
- The ability to store and recall helps us put things in order and perspective.

PROCESSING SPEED
- Ability to process info with speed means your brain is effective.
- It depends on the expanse of your knowledge and experience.
- Educators believe exposure to different scenarios and experiences can create the brain's capacity for processing speed.
- Neuroscientists think that well developed neural networks can achieve better processing speed.

- To fully use these skills, go beyond merely equipping your child with knowledge
- The strength and weaknesses of our skillsets determine our successes and struggles
- Intelligence comes when we can combine all these skills to think and deduce efficiently and coherently through life

The Brain's Input-Process-Output Process

In all processing system, there is an **Input-Process-Output** (IPO) progression.

In a computer system:

Input	Process	Output
data	data processing by CPU (central processing unit)	results

In our biological system:

Input	Process	Output
food ingested	food processed and digested	extracted nutrients absorbed, waste disposed

The brain works the same. Take reading out loud for example:

Input	Process	Output
eyes see text **(attention)** visual cues sent to the brain **(visualisation)**	neurotransmitters produce electrochemical signals to neurons **(attention and visualisation)** info processing with perception and speech cortices **(logical reasoning and memory)**	the act of verbalising the text **(processing speed)**

Let us use the exercise in Chapter 3 to understand the typical IPO process of your child.

We have red balls in 1 basket and white balls in another basket. Find out how many red balls and white balls are there?

2 equations:

1) If we take 1 red ball and 1 white ball out from the baskets each time, eventually, the red ball basket will be empty, and there will be 50 white balls left in the other basket.

2) If we take 1 red ball and 3 white balls out from the baskets each time, eventually, the white ball basket will be empty, and there will be 50 red balls left in the other basket.

In a gist, this is what happens during the IPO process of solving the above exercise.

1. The **attention** ability enables your child to read through the puzzle's preamble and 2 equations.
2. The **visual** ability enables your child to retain the read information in a relevant format with the power of brain visualisation.
3. The **logical reasoning** then allows you to work on the visualised baskets and apply a solution in an attempt to solve the problem.
4. The **memory** ability allows your child to remember and continually apply different possible solutions to work on the scenario.
5. The **processing speed** ability mobilises your child the appropriate emotional or physical response relevant to the comprehension of the problem.

MathBrain uses the above process of solving problems as the basis to drive children through the 5 brain abilities building activities and subsequently solving problems using these abilities, all in a fun approach for effectiveness.

In general, the primary functions of the **5 brain abilities** throughout a standard **Input-Process-Output** progression is explained in the following diagram.

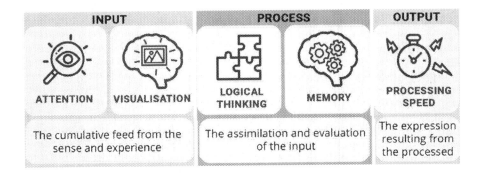

Putting the above schematics together, in short, we can summarise that

- The more the brain is exposed to relevant experiences or influences, the stronger the brain cells network that executes these skills
- The more the brain builds its abilities, the processing system becomes better; and one becomes smarter and more intelligent in dealing with all things in life
- This process is commonly known as brain-based learning, simply put, learning through how the brain works
- **MathBrain** by **BrainThink Learning** is based on this concept

With these understandings, as a parent or educator, you shall now have the power to implement targeted techniques to harness the brainpower of your children. With the advent of the latest scientific discoveries, brain-based learning should be the way forward for our next generation.

The Path to BrainThink Learning

Let's examine the differences between the commonly practised rote learning and BrainThink learning, which many labels as holistic education.

Rote Learning

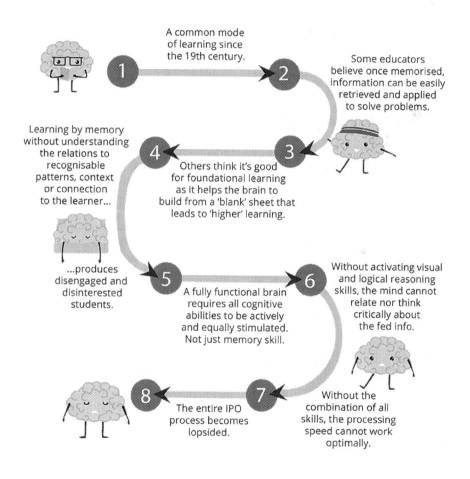

A common mode of learning since the 19th century.

Some educators believe once memorised, information can be easily retrieved and applied to solve problems.

Learning by memory without understanding the relations to recognisable patterns, context or connection to the learner...

Others think it's good for foundational learning as it helps the brain to build from a 'blank' sheet that leads to 'higher' learning.

...produces disengaged and disinterested students.

A fully functional brain requires all cognitive abilities to be actively and equally stimulated. Not just memory skill.

Without activating visual and logical reasoning skills, the mind cannot relate nor think critically about the fed info.

The entire IPO process becomes lopsided.

Without the combination of all skills, the processing speed cannot work optimally.

A newspaper survey in a South East Asian country poll found:

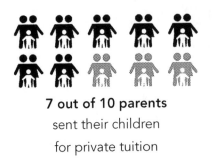

7 out of 10 parents
sent their children
for private tuition

Nearly **40%**
of preschool children
have **private tutors** in
**Mathematics
& English**

ONLY 1/3 of them make noticeable gains in their school results.
A low achievement results through the rote learning approach.

This raises the following questions:

- **What happens after the school exams?**

- **Would they know how to solve new problems?**

- **Are they able to effectively apply what they learn in problem-solving?**

BrainThink Learning

BrainThink Learning is based on **Input-Process-Output** (Nature) and **Curiosity-Explore-Test-Repeat-Master** (Nurture) to build your child's cognitive skills.

Based on how your child's brain physically develops and works, the BrainThink activities allow your child to exercise and strengthen all 5 brain abilities.

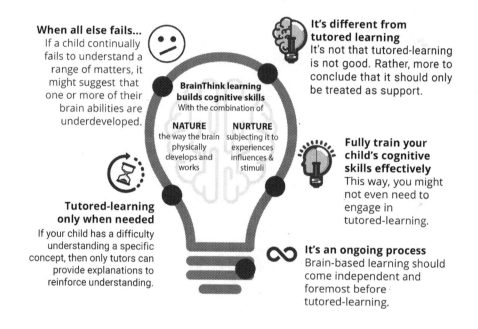

When all else fails...
If a child continually fails to understand a range of matters, it might suggest that one or more of their brain abilities are underdeveloped.

It's different from tutored learning
It's not that tutored-learning is not good. Rather, more to conclude that it should only be treated as support.

BrainThink learning builds cognitive skills
With the combination of
NATURE the way the brain physically develops and works
NURTURE subjecting it to experiences influences & stimuli

Fully train your child's cognitive skills effectively
This way, you might not even need to engage in tutored-learning.

Tutored-learning only when needed
If your child has a difficulty understanding a specific concept, then only tutors can provide explanations to reinforce understanding.

It's an ongoing process
Brain-based learning should come independent and foremost before tutored-learning.

Through **BrainThink Learning**'s play-to-learn programmes, the activities are specially designed to trigger your child's curiosity that allows them to continually explore, test, and repeat their problem-solving methods with interests.

As such, assessing your child's **5 brain abilities** is a good start for you to understand your child's cognitive skills and to provide the suitable education programmes.

Starting BrainThink Learning with the 5 Brain Abilities Assessment

If scientists are confident of being able to heal injured brains by working on the brain's architecture and re-conditioning a person's cognitive skills; imagine what we can achieve by training a healthy brain!

Many agree that the best time to maximise learning is during childhood. Children learn best before their circuits are fully formed when the brain is laying the foundation in its formation of neural networks. Research shows that early talkers make good readers. Children who explore the world with a mathematical bias make good mathematicians. Also, those who learn music at an early age have larger auditory cortices. We, as parents, know that the younger the age, the faster they absorb anything taught to them.

BrainThink Learning is an educational approach that is based on practical and behavioural examples. From all that is explained above, it seems clear that experiences and curiosities lead the brain's growth. An effective educator would raise interests with relevant scenarios to target the brain abilities, encourage the child to be inquisitive to experience, relate, apply, and stimulate the brain's operational process.

There is a myriad of **Play-Think-and-Learn** programmes, a variety of activities to stir the curiosities and many lessons to encourage experimentations and repetitions. All these lead to the all-important 'capture'. However, REAL capture can only be achieved if the education is targeted, strategic and purposeful, the crux of **BrainThink Learning**.

The more we can match a child's needs, the better we can provide them with quality **BrainThink Learning**. To achieve this, as with any approach to solving problems, we first need to identify the issues at hand. We need to understand our child's individual 5 brain abilities, identify their strengths and weaknesses, then ascertain the focus and objectives to find the correct techniques for each personality.

Matching a child's needs for quality education with 5 Brain Abilities Assessment

With a specialisation to promote this branch of learning, borne from a passion for effective education, parents are encouraged to use the **5 Brain Abilities Assessment** (5BA) to evaluate your child's 5 brain abilities, which will enable you to guide your child into powerful learning.

The 5 Brain Abilities Assessment is a simple test that takes less than an hour, which can be done individually or in a group.

5BA ASSESSMENT

DURATION	Less than 1 hour
# OF PAX	Individual or group

What are being assessed?

Attention, visual and memory abilities by image recognition

Memory and logical reasoning through hand-eye coordination activities

Logical reasoning though pattern recognition

Some examples of unbiased ability evaluations...

Evaluating your child's attention span and power of resilience towards completing a task (Attention ability)

Ascertaining your child's potential for imagination to interpret information (Visual ability)

Determing your child's power to retain and recall (Memory skill)

Finding the boundaries to the child's reasoning and deduction skills (Logical Reasoning ability)

Discovering gaps that may limit their thinking process (Processing Speed ability)

The Assessment Results include ...

A practical report, beyond mere grades that interprets and explains the findings

Recommendations of home-help or centre-led techniques to improve your child's weaknesses and capitalise on their strengths

Summary

The Benefits of 5 Brain Abilities Assessment to Parents & Educators

The 5 Brain Abilities (5BA) Assessment is a valuable tool to start your child on the way to BrainThink learning—a learning method that is not hindered by unrelated drill and memory work with relentless tuition sessions.

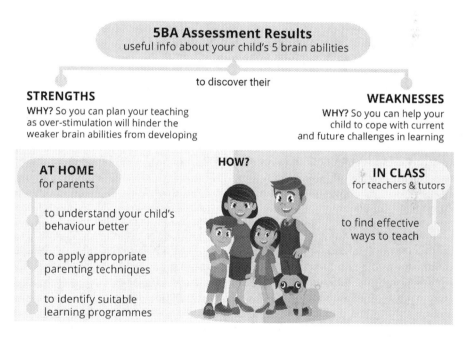

5BA Assessment Results
useful info about your child's 5 brain abilities

to discover their

STRENGTHS
WHY? So you can plan your teaching as over-stimulation will hinder the weaker brain abilities from developing

WEAKNESSES
WHY? So you can help your child to cope with current and future challenges in learning

HOW?

AT HOME
for parents

to understand your child's behaviour better

to apply appropriate parenting techniques

to identify suitable learning programmes

IN CLASS
for teachers & tutors

to find effective ways to teach

BrainThink Learning will create a journey for a happy childhood with meaningful and guided learning achieved in a healthy, happy and free environment.

What does it take?

Just approximately 45 to 60 minutes of your time to discover your child's 5 Brain Abilities. Guide your child to take the test today! Discover the world of opportunities to improve for your child.

Visit this website to learn more about the 5 Brain Abilities Assessment at https://www.5brain.org and sign up to have access to:

1. The full version of the 5 Brain Abilities Assessment*

   a) Select: Yes, I have the "MathBrain by BrainThink Learning" book

   b) Fill in ISBN number 9781-5437-49809 OR 9781-5437-49786, location of purchase and receipt of purchase.

2. A detailed report of your child's 5 Brain Abilities report

*Subject to change without notice

Disclaimer: This assessment is a guide for parents and educators to know and help their children's learning processes only. This is not a medical assessment nor medical advice. Authors, publisher and copyright owner of 5 Brain Abilities Assessment give no warranty and accept no responsibility or liability for the accuracy or the completeness of the information and materials contained in the assessment.

CHAPTER 9

UNLIMITED POSSIBILITIES:
The Practical Applications
of Vedic Math

**SIMPLY POSSIBLE – How Learners Can Enjoy and Yet,
Get MORE out of Math**

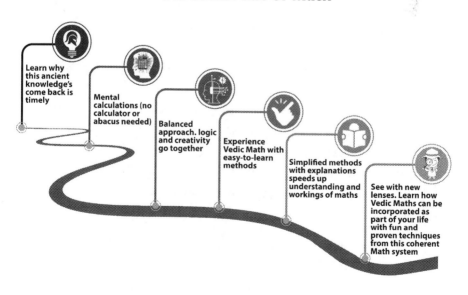

Learn why this ancient knowledge's come back is timely

Mental calculations (no calculator or abacus needed)

Balanced approach. logic and creativity go together

Experience Vedic Math with easy-to-learn methods

Simplified methods with explanations speeds up understanding and workings of maths

See with new lenses. Learn how Vedic Maths can be incorporated as part of your life with fun and proven techniques from this coherent Math system

Old in New, yet Old is Gold

Vedic Math is a valuable ancient system of math that has since found its place right back into present time. In modern times, we are always looking for efficient ways to solve problems .in a speedy, yet reliable and accurate manner. Vedic Math, derived from the ancient Sanskrit texts, meets that need perfectly. Reconstructed between 1911 and 1918 by the Indian scholar, Sri Bharati Krishna Tirthaji, it is a complete and coherent math system that applies to all areas of pure and applied math.

With sutras providing the rules or core principles, one can find and use a variety of methods that are easy to understand. This is because Vedic Math sutras work in tandem with the natural pathways of the brain. The methods are easy to assimilate and work on in contrast to conventional math.

Like the word "sutra" itself, which means "thread", the sutras enable individuals to connect through a web of math concepts like threads of logic, hence the more natural flow of working out calculations.

Creative Math

When someone brings up the matter or for the fact, any matter on math, creativity is not a word that is usually associated or linked with it. Creativity is underrated in the world of math. However, in contrast to the conventional perception of doing math, learning Vedic Math opens a new dimension of creativity in a subject most often thought to be uncreative and unimaginative.

Its flexibility and varied methods do not require one to memorize fixed steps to solving a problem. Rather, a student can decide for themselves the best solution to apply based on the problem at hand.

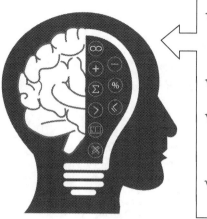

√ The methods have a wide range or versatility in terms of its application.

√ Methods are reversible.

√ No tedious workings or using a combination of functions as methods are concise.

√ Speedy and efficient development of problem-solving skills.

Be Empowered

Once you and/or your child learn and practise the Vedic principles, you will realise how much and how well you can do math. This new sense of empowerment gives you the confidence to use and rely on your own abilities to solve everyday mathematical problems. Equipped with Vedic Math, you are actually nurturing your MathBrain qualities. Tap into the greatness of your brain and put away your calculators!

You and/or your child will not be needing calculators now that you have turned on and tuned your brain to the dynamic frequency of Vedic Math, **MathBrain** style! Gone are the days of dreading calculations. From now on, you and/or your child can have a fresh start in math and will likely be looking for and welcoming new challenges to do math using the 5 Brain Abilities.

Apply, Enjoy, Master!

Nevertheless, there is no limit to the number of solutions as you can devise them for your own needs once you know and understand the methods. As you will learn, Vedic Math is not rigid. When you learn to recognize the patterns in numbers and various elements in math concepts, you learn to link them and form connections.

From there, you can further develop the methods taught into something based on your needs and circumstances, and even create or use opportunities to practise this invaluable knowledge with family and friends.

Mind over Matter

Besides, there is unlimited creativity you and/or your child can apply into Vedic Math, whether it is visualizing a pattern, a question, a solution or even to create your own methods! This book's function is to introduce you and/or your child to this powerful and effective subject. You and/or your child will empower yourselves once you know; try out the mathematical problem samples provided and experience it on your own using your own abilities ways to solve math problems using the science of Vedic Math.

Why Vedic Math?

- Complementary knowledge of children's conventional learning in schools.
- Eliminate baseless fear of Math.
- Create a fun and stimulating journey of learning.
- Allow young learners to engage with their creativity by exploring the flexible and simple sutras of Vedic Math.
- Opening doors to experimental learning of mathematics.

Children will not be confused by learning another method of calculation. In fact, this can be an alternative method to their existing knowledge of math and provide them with a greater advantage in understanding of numbers with this added knowledge, adding up to outstanding numeracy skills. We hope Vedic Math to can take you and your child to a new level of self-empowerment and instil MathBrain qualities in yourself, your child, family, educators and students!

Life Lessons through Vedic Math

Math is **essential** in life because it is used to perform
many different daily tasks.

On a daily basis, we receive various data that must be organized and absorbed before we can make decisions. Routine daily activities from telling time, reading your vehicle's odometer to determining the best deals at a store, and the ability to count money and receive the correct change are important mathematical problems people solve daily.

Other strategic decisions in one's life which involve some math skills include saving and investing money, planning for retirement, choosing insurance and calculating expenses. Not only that, but almost every profession requires some form of math.

Essentially, learning is one thing but applying the knowledge you gain to real situations or teaching others enables you to optimise assimilation of your knowledge into a subject matter. Once you get started, you will enjoy it and having **MathBrain** through **BrainThink Learning** will become a way of life. Just as it is said, any mastery is but a matter of practice. With practices, understanding and self-mastery naturally improve. The next few chapters are an introduction of elementary Vedic Math sutras for beginners.

Math that Anyone Can Do

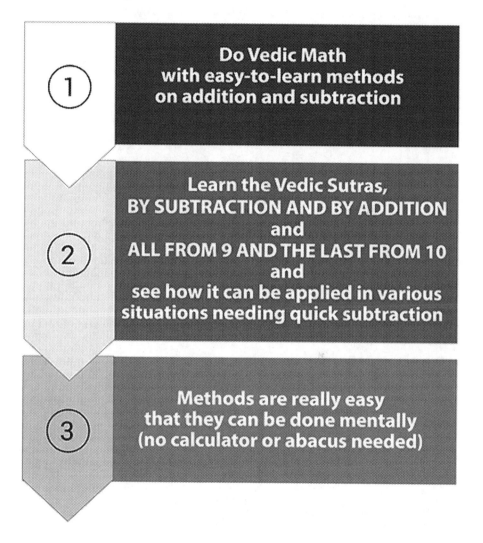

Now, let us get started with some amazingly simple additions and subtractions, Vedic Math style!

Check Your Bill

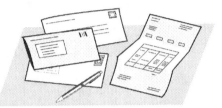

Use this easy technique of adding numbers to check your bank statement or supermarket bill.

The usual way to add numbers works from right to left and so is not useful for mental math.

Numbers are written and spoken from **left to right** and so, it is easier to work from **left to right** especially when doing it in your head.

* 34 + 52 = <u>86</u>

This is easy to do from left to right.

We add 3 and 5 to get 8.

And we add 4 and 2 to get 6.

So, the answer is **86**

Just practise one or two:

1) 44 + 34 =   2) 52 + 37 =   3) 246 + 642 =

Now, suppose that there is **a carry figure,**

* 76 + 86 = 162

The figures on the left add up to 7 + 8 = 15.

The figures on the right add up to 6 + 6 = 12.

> » 15 12 = (15 + 1) 2 = **162**

Now as 12 is a 2-figure number the 1 will be carried over to make the 15 into 16, giving **162.**

This is easy to do in your head – for any 2-figure number carry the left-hand figure to the left.

* 373 + 474 = 847

First, we get 3 + 4 = 7.

Then we get 7 + 7 =14.

Finally, we get 3 + 4 = 7,

which gives 7 14 7 = (7+1) 4 7 = **847**

Try these:

1) 44 + 77 =

2) 87 + 86 =

3) 28 + 38 =

4) 65 + 56 =

5) 464 + 262 =

6) 773 + 883 =

7) 177 + 277 =

Check Your Change

Using BY SUBTRACTION AND ADDITION you can quickly check

Suppose you offer $50 for something that costs $19.

* 50 – 19 = 31

To take 19 from 50, we note that 19 is close to 20, so we take away 20 from 50 (to get 30) and add 1 back on.

*Similarly, in **73 – 48** we decide to take 50 away from 73 and then add 2 back on.

73 – 48 = 73 – 50 + 2 = **<u>25</u>**

⌐ Try these:

1) 62 – 36 =   2) 84 – 48 =   3) 71 – 27 =

4) 43 – 16 =   5) 55 – 28 =

Amaze Your Friends

Use the formula ALL FROM 9 AND THE LAST 10 to amaze your friends with instant subtractions.

For example, **1000 - 357 = 643**

We simply take each figure in 357 from 9 except the last figure from 10:

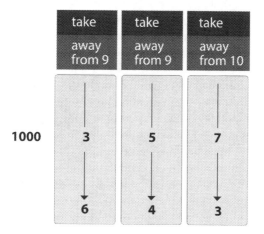

So, the answer is **643.**

And that's all there is to it!

This always works for subtractions from numbers consisting of a 1 followed by noughts: 100; 1000; 10,000 etc.

* Similarly, **10,000 - 1049 = <u>8951</u>**

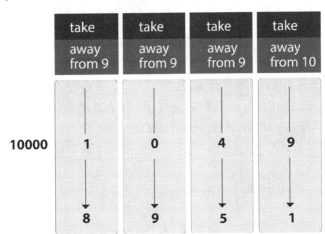

	take	take	take	take
	away from 9	away from 9	away from 9	away from 10
10000	1	0	4	9
	8	9	5	1

* For 1000 - 83 in which we have more zeros than figures in the numbers being subtracted we simply suppose that 83 is 083.

So, 1000 - 83 becomes 1000 - 083 = **<u>917</u>**

Try some yourself:

1) 1000 - 777   =

2) 1000 - 283   =

3) 1000 - 505   =

4) 10,000 - 2345 =

5) 10,000 - 9876 =

6) 10,000 - 1101 =

7) 100 - 57   =

8) 1000 - 57   =

9) 10,000 - 321 =

10) 10,000 - 38 =

In the Shop

This astonishing method for multiplying numbers is so easy because it works from left to right

* Suppose you buy something for $3.33 and you give a $10 note. How much change would you expect to get?

You just apply ALL FROM 9 AND THE LAST FROM 10 to the $3.33 and you get **$6.67**.

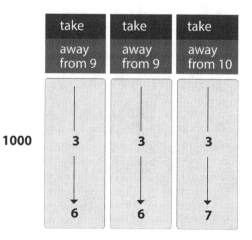

	take	take	take
	away from 9	away from 9	away from 10
1000	3	3	3
	6	6	7

More examples:

* \$ 10 - \$ 2.30 = <u>\$ 7.70</u>

Here "the last" is the 3 as zero does not count.

So, we take 2 from 9 and 3 from 10.

> » (9 - 2) (10 - 3) (0 - 0) = **770**

* Similarly, \$ 100 - \$ 45.25 = <u>\$ 54.75</u>

> » (9 - 4) (9 - 5) (9 - 2) (10 - 5) = **5475**

Try some yourself:

1) \$ 10 - \$ 7.77 =   2) \$ 10 - \$ 4.44 =

3) \$ 10 - \$ 6.36 =   4) \$ 10 - \$ 5.67 =

5) \$ 100 - \$ 84.24 =   6) \$ 100 - \$ 31.33 =

CHAPTER 10

Tables Magic

What can you learn from this chapter?

- Find out how to do Multiplications using Vedic Math methods in this chapter!

- Learn the Sutra, VERTICALLY AND CROSSWISE, and see how it simplifies multiplication in 3 steps!

- Mentally work out 2-digits multiplications with easy-to-learn methods

- Magic of 11

Tables Magic

**Don't know your tables of multiplication?
Don't worry! In this system, you do not
need to memorise at all.**

*Suppose you need 8 x 7

8 is 2 below 10 and 7 is 3 below 10.
Think of it like this:

```
        8  -2

   x  7  -3
   _____

        5  6
```

The answer is **56**

The diagram below shows how you get it.

```
        8    -2

   x  7      -3
   _____

        5    6
```

You subtract crosswise: 8 – 3 or 7 – 2 to get 5, the first figure of the answer.
And you multiply vertically: 2 x 3 to get 6, the last figure of the answer.
That's all you do!

Why?

8 x 7

= (10 - 2) x (10 - 3)

= 10 x 10 - 10 x 3 - 10 x 2 + 2 x 3

= (10 - 3 - 2) 10 + 2 x 3 ← | Unit place |

| 7 – 2 Or 8 – 3, to get **5**, which is at **10s place** |

So, the answer is **56**.

Think about how far each single-digit number is from 10, subtract one number's deficiency from 10, and then use either one of the numbers to subtract crosswise the number to get the answer's Tens and then to get the answer's Units, multiply the deficiencies together, as below.

* 7 x 6 = 42

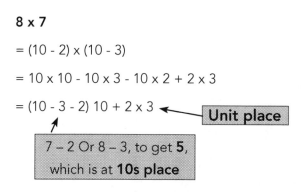

```
      7   -3
  x   6   -4
  ─────────────
      3   12 = 42
```

Here there is a carry: the 1 in 12 goes over to make the 3 into 4.

» 3   12 = (3 + 1) 2 = **42**

Multiply these:

a) 8   b) 9   c) 8   d) 7   e)   9   f)   6

  x 8   x 7   x 9   x 7   x 9   x 6

In the Supermarket

Why not check your sums by this fascinating method using digit sums

*Suppose you want to know the cost of 6 bananas at 73 cents each.

* 73 x 6 = <u>438 cents</u>

We first multiply the 7 by 6 to get 42.

We then multiply the 3 by 6 to get 18.

» 42 18 = 4 (2 + 1) 8 = **438**

The 1 in the 18 is mentally carried to the 42 to make it 43.

So, any double-figure outcome at the units involves carrying the first figure to the left and adding it on.

More examples:

A) 234 x 7 = <u>1638</u>

We get 2 x 7 = 14

Then, 3 x 7 = 21

Finally, 4 x 7 = 28

14 21 28 » 1 (4 + 2) (1 + 2) 8 = **1638**

B) 282 x 4 = <u>1128</u>

First, we get 2 x 4 = 8 = 08 (2 digits)

Then, 8 x 4 = 32 (2 digits)

Finally, 2 x 4 = 08 (2 digits)

As 08   32   08 » 0 (8 + 3) (2 + 0) 8 = **1128**

C) 43 x 7 = 28 21 » 2 (8 + 2) 1

» 2 (10) 1 » (2 + 1) 0 1 » **301** (28 becomes 30)

Try a few of these:

1) 56 x 6 =	2) 43 x 4 =	3) 77 x 5 =
4) 88 x 9 =	5) 66 x 7 =	6) 18 x 8 =
7) 45 x 7 =	8) 444 x 3 =	9) 383 x 7 =

Have A Break

During break time at school or in the office, try out this elegant way of multiplying numbers using a simple pattern.

* 21 x 23 = <u>483</u>

This is normally called long multiplication, but actually, the answer can be written straight down using the VERTICALLY AND CROSSWISE formula.

There are 3 steps:

a) Multiply vertically on the left: 2 x 2 = 4

b) Multiply crosswise and add: (2 x 3) + (1 x 2) = 8

c) Multiply vertically on the right: 1 x 3 = 3

And that's all there is to it.

* Similarly, 61 x 31 = 1891

```
                    6      1
        x           3      1
     ─────────────────────────
        1     8     9      1
```

» 6 x 3 = **18** ; (6 x 1) + (3 x 1) = **9** ; 1 x 1 = **1**

Try these:

a)   1 4   b)   2 2   c)   2 1   d)   2 1   e)   3 2

    x 2 1   x 3 1   x 3 1   x 2 2   x 2 2

Why?

* 21 x 23 = 483

Traditional way: Vertically and Crosswise:

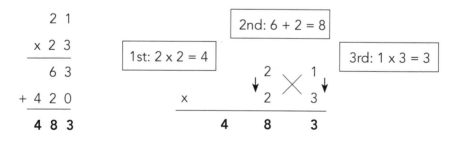

Note that the first figure is obtained by multiplying 2 x 2 = 4.

The second figure is by adding 6 (2 x 3) and 2 (1 x 2), to get 8.

The last figure is by multiplying 1 x 3 = 3.

* We can summarize the steps by using VERTICALLY AND CROSSWISE which is shown above, on the right, which show similarities with the traditional method.

At the Post Office

Multiply any 2-figure number together by mere mental arithmetic!

If you want 21 stamps at 26 cents each, you can easily find the total price in your head.

There were no carries in the method given on the previous page. These only need one extra small step, however.

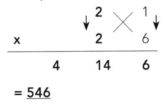

= <u>546</u>

* 21 x 26 = 546

The method is the same as the previous page except that we get a 2- figure number, 14, in the middle step, (2 x 6) + (2 x 1) = 14, so the 1 is carried over to the left (4 becomes 5).

So, 21 stamps at 26 cents each cost **$5.46.**

Practise a few:

a) 2 1	b) 2 3	c) 3 2	d) 4 2	e) 7 1
x 4 7	x 4 3	x 5 3	x 3 2	x 7 2

More example:

* 33 x 44 = 1452

There may be more than one carry in the sum:

2nd: 12 + 12 = 24

1st: 3 x 4 = 12		3rd: 3 x 4 = 12

$$
\begin{array}{ccc}
 & 3 \times 3 \\
\times & 4 \quad 4 \\
\hline
12 & 24 & 12
\end{array}
$$

» 1 (2+2) (4+1) 2 » **1452**

Practise a few:

f) 2 2	g) 3 2	h) 3 1	i) 4 4	j) 5 4
x 5 6	x 5 4	x 7 2	x 5 3	x 6 4

In fact, any two numbers, no matter how big they are, can be multiplied in one line with this method.

Impress Your Parents

Multiplying a number by 11 is incredibly
easy — astonish your parents and friends with this!

To multiply any 2-figure number by 11, we add the neighbouring
numbers.

Example 1:

* 26 x 11 = __286__

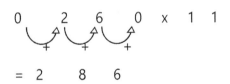

Since there are no numbers besides 2 and 6, we write 0 to indicate.

1st : add 0 + 2 = 2 (neighbour of 2 is nothing)

2nd: add 2 + 6 = 8 (add 2 neighbours)

3rd : add 6 + 0 = 6 (neighbour of 6 is nothing)

The answer is **286.**

Note that the outer figures in 286 are the 26 being multiplied by 11.

Example 2:

* 72 x 11 = 792

1st » nothing (0) + 7 = 7
2nd » 7 + 2 = 9
3rd » 2 + nothing (0) = 2

So the answer is **792**

Try multiply by 11:

1) 43 x 11   2) 81 x 11   3) 15 x 11

4) 44 x 11   5) 11 x 11

Example 3:

* 77 x 11 = 847

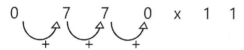

This involves a carry figure because 7 + 7 = 14.

= (7+1) 4 7 = **847**

Try multiply by 11:

6) 88 x 11   7) 84 x 11   8) 48 x 11

9) 73 x 11   10) 56 x 11

"Can we apply this method to longer numbers?" You may ask. Definitely.

Example 3:

* 234 x 11 = <u>**2574**</u>

The same rule of adding to the neighbouring numbers applies.

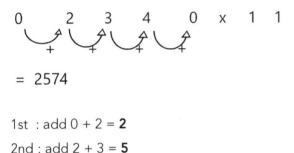

= 2574

1st : add 0 + 2 = **2**
2nd : add 2 + 3 = **5**
3rd : add 3 + 4 = **7**
4th : add 4 + 0 = **4**

CHAPTER 11

Interesting Patterns

What can you learn from this chapter?

- Learn about Digit Sums

- Learn more applications of the Sutra, VERTICALLY AND CROSSWISE in multiplication

- The Nine-Point Circle, multiplication tables' pattern on the circle and other useful applications

- Digit Sums as a Checking Tool

- Mental multiplication over a 100!

Here are some brilliant Vedic Math methods you would not want to miss out on.

On a car journey, get the children to find the digit sum of car number plates.

On the Motorway

Any number of any size can always be reduced to a single figure by adding its digits.

* For example, 42 has two digits which add up to 6.
We say "the digit sum of 42 is 6".

* The digit sum of 413 is 8 because 4 + 1 + 3 = 8.

* For 20511 the digit sum is 9.

Try a few:

1) 34   2) 61   3) 303

4) 3041   5) 21212

* Now suppose we want the digit sum of **417**.
4 + 1 + 7 = 12.

But as 12 is a 2-figure number we add its digits to get 3: 1 + 2 = 3.

We could write **417** -> 4 + 1 + 7 -> 12 -> 1 + 2 -> 3

Another example:

* Single digit sum of 737 -> 7 + 3 + 7 -> 17 -> 1 + 7 -> 8

We simply add the digits in the number and add again if necessary. This is simple and one of its uses is in checking sums, as we will see.

Find the digit sum for each of the following:

1) 85   2) 38   3) 77

4) 99   5) 616   6) 7654

The Nine-Point Circle

Since all numbers, no matter how long, can be reduced to a single figure, as such, every number will find its place on the nine-point circle:

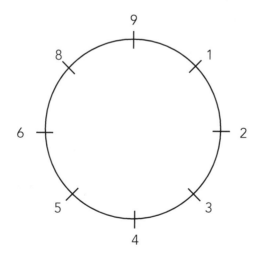

The circle shows the numbers from 1 to 9 and continuing to number around the circle would put 10 at the same place as 1.

11 would be at the same place as 2 and so on as shown below:

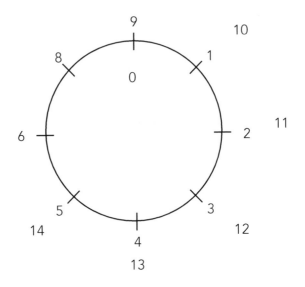

Note also that 0 is at the same place as 9 because, numbering backwards around the circle, 0 comes before 1.

Even the multiplication tables show a certain pattern on the circle. For instance, the multiples of 2 are 2, 4, 6, 8, 10, 12,14, 16, ... when you reduce them using digit sums, we get 2, 4, 6, 8, 1, 3, 5, 7, ...

To get the pattern of the two times table, we start with 2 on the nine-point circle and draw a straight line to 4, then from 4, draw a line to 6 and so on until the pattern repeats itself.

So, all the numbers will have their place somewhere around this circle.

Now, looking at the last circle, the digit sum of 10 is 1, and 10 is next to 1 on the circle.

The digit sum of 11 is 2, and 11 is next to 2... and so on.

To find which branch of the circle a number is on, we simply find its digit sum.

* For example, the digit sum of 34 is 7 so 34 will come on the '7 branch'.

You could check this by continuing to number around the circle until you get 34.

* 77 will be on the '5 branch' as 77 » 7 + 7 = 14 » 1 + 4 = 5.

Put these numbers on the correct branch of the circle:

1) 88   2) 373   3) 555   4) 67348

In Math Lessons

Why not check your sums by this
fascinating method using digit sums

Suppose you want to check that the addition of the sum below is correct.

$$
\begin{array}{r}
4\ 3 \\
+\ \ 3\ 2 \\
\hline
7\ 5
\end{array}
$$

We find the digit sum of 43, 32 and 75 and check that the first two digits sums add up to the third digit sum:

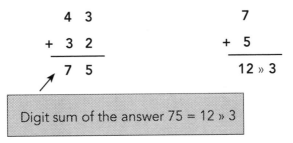

Digit sum of the answer 75 = 12 » 3

Digit sum of the answer 75 = 12 » 3

The digit sums are shown on the right. 7 + 5 = 12 » 1+2 = 3 This indicates that the answer is correct.

All sums, even the most complex, can be checked in this way.

Check the following sums and find out which are **wrong**:

1)	5 6	2)	8 3	3)	7 7	4)	5 4 5
	+ 8 8		+ 3 8		+ 6 9		+ 2 7 3
	1 4 4		1 2 1		1 5 9		8 1 8

It is worth noting (in case you want to check subtraction sums using the nine-point circle) that in digit sums for 7 – 5 = 2, 6 – 6 = 0 and so on, but

3-4=8. You can see this on the circle by starting at 3 and going 4 jumps backwards around the circle.

Or, alternatively, you can add 9 to the 3 so that 3 - 4 becomes (3+9) – 4 = 12 – 4, which is 8.

At the Party

At a party, surprise your friends with this spectacular way of multiplying large numbers together from your mind.

Here's how to use the formula VERTICALLY AND CROSSWISE for multiplying numbers close to 100.

This follows on from the previous page.

* Suppose you want to multiply 88 by 98.

Not easy, you might think. But with VERTICALLY AND CROSSWISE you can put the answer straight down, using the same method as on the last page.

Both 88 and 98 are close to 100.

88 is 12 below 100 and 98 is 2 below 100.

You can imagine the sum set out like this:

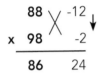

```
    88  ╲  -12  ↓
        ╳
x   98  ╱   -2
   ─────────────
    86     24
```

As before the **86** comes from subtracting crosswise:

88 – 2 = 86   OR   98 – 12 = 86

(You can subtract, either way, you will always get the same answer)

And the 24 in the answer is just 12 x 2. (Multiply vertically)

So, 88 x 98 = <u>8624</u>

This is easy, it is just mental arithmetic.

⌐ Try some:

a)   8 7   b)   8 8   c)   7 7   d)   9 3

      x 9 8   x 9 7   x 9 8   x 9 6
      ─────────   ─────────   ─────────   ─────────

e)   9 4   f)   6 4

      x 9 2   x 9 9
      ─────────   ─────────

Exercise Your Brain Cells

While waiting in a queue why not exercise your brain cells by multiplying numbers just over 100.

* 103 x 104 = <u>10712</u>

$$\begin{array}{r} 103 \\ 104 \end{array} \quad X \quad \begin{array}{l} +3 \\ +4 \end{array}$$

$$\overline{\quad 107 \quad 12 \quad}$$

(103 = 100 + 3; 104 = 100 + 4)

The answer is in two parts: 107 and 12

1st part: 103 + 4 = 107   OR   104 + 3 = 107

2nd part : 3 x 4 = 12

Why?

103 x 104

= (100 + 3) x (100 + 4)

= 100 x 100 + 100 x 4 + 100 x 3 + 3 x 4

= (100 + 4 + 3) 100 + 3 x 4   ⬅ | Unit place |

⬆

| 104 + 3 Or 103 + 4, to get
107, which is 100s place |

So, the answer is **10712**.

Another example:

* Similarly, **107 x 106 = 11342**

$$\begin{array}{rr} 107 & +7 \\ 106 & +6 \\ \hline \mathbf{113} & \mathbf{42} \end{array}$$

(107 = 100 + 7; 106 = 100 + 6)

1st part: 107 + 6 = 113   OR   106 + 7 = **113**

2nd part : 7 x 6 = **42**

Again, just mental arithmetic.

Try a few:

1) 102 x 107

2) 106 x 103

3) 104 x 104

4) 109 x 108

5) 101 x 123

6) 103 x 102

CHAPTER 12

Human Calculator

What can you learn from this chapter?

- Learn the Sutra, BY ONE MORE THAN THE ONE BEFORE to do squaring for numbers ending in 5, in a flash!

- More easy-to-learn multiplication method

- Find out what else the Sutra, VERTICALLY AND CROSSWISE can do to add and subtract fractions

- Dividing by 9

   Mental power rules, any day!

On A Walk

Out walking with your friends, show them this quick way to square numbers that end with 5 using the formula **BY ONE MORE THAN THE ONE BEFORE.**

* 75^2 = <u>**5625**</u>

75^2 means 75 x 75

The answer is in two parts: **56** and **25**. The last part is always 25.

The first part is the first number, 7, multiplied by the number "one more", which is 8.

So, 7 x (7+1) = 7 x 8 = 56

$$7 \ 5^2 = 56 \quad 25$$

* Similarly, **85^2** = <u>**7225**</u> because 8 x 9 = 72

So, 8 x (8+1) = 8 x 9 = **72**, (5 x 5) = **25**

⌐ Try these:

1) 45^2 2) 65^2 3) 95^2 4) 35^2 5) 15^2

At the Office

Show your colleagues in the office this beautiful method for multiplying numbers where the first figures are the same and the last figures add up to 10.

* 32 x 38 = <u>1216</u>

Both numbers here have 3 in the tens place and the figures in unit place (2 and 8) adds up to 10.

1st part: We just multiply 3 by 4 ("one more" than 3) to get **12**

2nd part: multiply the last figures: 2 x 8 = **16**.

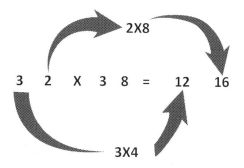

Why ?

Explanation:

32 x 38

$$= (30 + 2) \times (30 + 8)$$

$$= 30 \times 30 + 8 \times 30 + 2 \times 30 + 2 \times 8$$

$$= 30 \times 30 + (8+2) \times 30 + 2 \times 8$$

$$= 30 \times 30 + 10 \times 30 + 2 \times 8$$

$$= 30 \times (30 + 10) + 2 \times 8$$

$$= 3 \times (3 + 1) \times 100 + 2 \times 8 \longleftarrow \boxed{\text{Unit place}}$$

$$\boxed{3 \times 4 \text{ ("one more" than 3), which is } \textbf{100s place}}$$

$$= (3 \times 4) \times 100 + 2 \times 8$$

$$= 1200 + 16$$

$$= \textbf{1216}$$

Practise some:

1) 43 x 47 =   2) 24 x 26 =

3) 62 x 68 =   4) 17 x 13 =

5) 59 x 51 =   6) 77 x 73 =

Show Your Child

Show your children this truly beautiful method of dividing by 9

Use VERTICALLY AND CROSSWISE and write the answer straight down.

$$\star \frac{2}{3} \; + \; \frac{1}{5} \; = \; \frac{10 + 3}{3 \times 5}$$

$$= \frac{13}{15}$$

Multiply crosswise and add to get the top of the answer:
2 x 5 = 10 and 1 x 3 = 3. Then 10 + 3 = 13

The bottom of the fraction is just 3 x 5 = 15.

$$\star \frac{5}{7} \; + \; \frac{3}{4} \; = \; \frac{20 + 21}{7 \times 4}$$

$$= \frac{41}{28}$$

$$= 1\frac{13}{28}$$

Subtracting is just as easy, multiply crosswise as before, but then subtract:*

$$* \ \frac{6}{7} \ - \ \frac{2}{3} \ = \ \frac{18 - 14}{7 \times 3}$$

$$= \ \frac{4}{21}$$

Try a few:

1) $\frac{4}{5} + \frac{1}{6}$

2) $\frac{1}{3} + \frac{1}{4}$

3) $\frac{2}{7} + \frac{2}{3}$

4) $\frac{4}{5} + \frac{1}{6}$

5) $\frac{1}{4} + \frac{1}{5}$

6) $\frac{8}{3} + \frac{9}{5}$

Delight Your Child

Show your this truly beautiful method of dividing by 9.

23 ÷ 9 = <u>2 remainder 5</u>

The first figure of 23 is 2

The remainder is just 2 and 3 added up ie 2 + 3 = 5

* 43 ÷ 9 = <u>4 remainder 7</u>

The first figure of 43 is 4,

and first add the second figure, 4+3 = 7 is the remainder – could it be easier?

Divide these by 9:

1) 61 ÷ 9 =   2) 33 ÷ 9 =   3) 44 ÷ 9 =

4) 53 ÷ 9 =   5) 80 ÷ 9 =

Longer numbers also are easy:

* 134 ÷ 9 = <u>14 remainder 8</u>

The answer consists of 1, 4 and 8.

1 is just the first figure of 134,

4 is the total of the first two figures 1 + 3 = 4

8 is the total of all three figures 1 + 3 + 4 = 8.

Divide these by 9:

6) 232 ÷ 9 =   7) 151 ÷ 9 =   8) 303 ÷ 9 =

9) 212 ÷ 9 =   10) 2121 ÷ 9 =

Improve Your Mind

On a long car journey why not improve
your mind by dividing the car numbers
by 9 using this remarkably easy method

This follows on from the previous page because these sums may have
carry figures.

* 842 ÷ 9 = 8 12 or (8+1) 2 remainder 14 = **92 remainder 14**
1st figure = 8
2nd figure = 8 + 4 = 12
3rd figure = 8 + 4 + 2 = 14

Actually, a remainder of 9 or more is not usually permitted because we
are trying to find how many 9's are in 842.

Since the remainder, 14, has one more 9 with 5 leftover,
the final answer will be 93 with the remainder of 5.

92 remainder 14 = 93 remainder 5

Divide these by 9:

1) 771 ÷ 9 =   2) 942 ÷ 9 =   3) 565 ÷ 9 =

4) 555 ÷ 9 =   5) 777 ÷ 9 =   6) 2382 ÷ 9 =

7) 7070 ÷ 9 =   8) 3076 ÷ 9 =

Answers

Chapter 9: Math That Anyone Can Do

Check Your Bill

1) 78   2) 89   3) 888

1) 121   2) 173   3) 66   4) 121

5) 726   6) 1656   7) 454

Check Your Change

1) 26   2) 36   3) 44   4) 27   5) 27

Amaze Your Friends

1) 223   2) 717   3) 495   4) 7655   5) 124

6) 8899   7) 43   8) 943   9) 9679   10) 9962

In the Shop

1) $2.23   2) $5.56   3) $3.64

4) $4.33   5) $15.76   6) $68.67

Chapter 10: Tables Magic

Tables Magic
a) 64   b) 63   c) 72

d) 49   e) 81   f) 36

In the Supermarket
1) 336   2) 172   3) 385   4) 792   5) 462

6) 144   7) 315   8) 121212 = 1332   9) 215621=2681

Have A Break
a) 294   b) 682   c) 651   d) 462   e) 672

At the Post Office
a) 987   b) 989   c) 1696   d) 1344   e) 5112

f) 1232   g) 1728   h) 2232   i) 2332   j) 3456

Impress Your Parents
1) 473   2) 891   3) 165   4) 484   5) 121

6) 968   7) 924   8) 528   9) 803   10) 616

Chapter 11: Interesting Patterns

On the Motorway
1) 7	2) 7	3) 6	4) 8	5) 8
1) 4	2) 2	3) 5	4) 9	5) 4
6) 4				

The Nine-Point Circle
1) 7	2) 4	3) 6	4) 1

In Math Lesson
1) correct   2) correct

3) wrong as 5+6 does not equal 3 in digit sum   4) correct

At the Party
a) 8526	b) 8536	c) 7546
d) 8928	e) 8648	f) 6336

Exercise Your Brain Cells
1) 10914	2) 10918	3) 10816	4) 11772

5) 12423   6) 10506 (we put 06, because 105 is in 100s place)

Chapter 12: Human Calculator

On A Walk
1) 2025   2) 4225   3) 9025   4) 1225   5) 225

At the Office
1) 2021   2) 624   3) 4216
4) 221   5) 3009   6) 5621

Show Your Child
1) $\frac{29}{30}$ 2) $\frac{7}{12}$ 3) $\frac{20}{21}$

4) $\frac{19}{30}$ 5) $\frac{1}{20}$ 6) $\frac{13}{15}$

Delight Your Child

1) 6 R7   2) 3 R6   3) 4 R8   4) 5 R8   5) 8 R8

6) 25 R7   7) 16 R7   8) 33 R6   9) 23 R5   10) 235 R6

Improve Your Mind

(1) 714 R 15 = 84 R15 = 85 R 6

(2) 913 R 15 = 103 R15 = 104 R6

(3) 511 R16 = 61 R16 = 62 R7

(4) 510 R15 = 60 R15 = 61 R6

(5) 714 R21 = 84 R21 = 86 R3

(6) 2513 R15 = 263 R15 = 264 R6

(7) 7714 R14 = 784 R14 = 785 R5

(8) 3310 R16 = 340 R16 = 341 R7

References

i.   Schwarzmueller, G., & Rinaldo, V. (2013). The importance of self-directed play. Kappa Delta Pi Record, 49(1), 37-41.

ii.   Tierney, A. L., & Nelson III, C. A. (2009). Brain development and the role of experience in the early years. Retrieved from https://www.ncbi. nlm.nih.gov.

iii.   University of North Carolina (1999). Early Learning, Later Success: The Abecedarian Study. Retrieved from http://fpg.unc.edu/

iv.   Pelligrini AD and Holmes RM (2006). The role of recess in primary school. In D.Singer, R. Golinkoff, & K. Hirsh-Pasek (Eds.), Play=learning: How play motivates and enhances children's cognitive and socio-emotional growth. New York: Oxford University Press.

v.   Symonds, P. W. (1939). The psychology of parent-child relationships. Oxford, England: Appleton-Century.

vi.   Mekarina, M., & Ningsih, Y. P. (2017, September). The Effects of Brain Based Learning Approach on Motivation and Students Achievement in Mathematics Learning. In Journal of Physics: Conference Series (Vol. 895, No. 1, p. 012057). IOP Publishing.

vii.   Roderick. J. Simonds, and Arnold B. Scheibel, "The Postnatal Development of the Motor Speech Area: A preliminary Study," Brain and Language, 37 (1989) 42-58.

viii.   Vasantha Kandasamy, W. B., & Smarandache, F. (2006). Vedic Mathematics : 'Vedic'or'Mathematics'--A Fuzzy and Neutrosophic Analysis.

BOOKS ON VEDIC MATHEMATICS BY

KENNETH WILLIAMS

Below is a selection of books available.
The full list and further details can be found at:
http://www.vedicmaths.org/shop/books

A Trillion Triangles

This book introduces trigonometry in an easy way that is very suitable for children from around grade 7. Children make and manipulate triangles and learn how to combine them. This leads on to more advanced work including the 4 new chapters on solution of right-angled triangles without a calculator.

Teacher's Manuals 1, 2, 3

Elementary Level – grades 3 to 7
Intermediate Level – grades 5 to 10
Advanced Level – grades 9 to 14

For teachers or parents of children who wish to learn the Vedic system and teach it.

The Art of Calculus

This is an introduction to Calculus, starting right at the beginning. The book shows highly unusual and simple methods for getting gradients and areas under curves without the usual confusing symbols and terminology.

The Cosmic Calculator Course

This course covers Key Stage 3 (age 11–14 years) of the National Curriculum for England and Wales, which will be similar to most other curricula.

Words can make or break a business.
That's why you need a copywriter.

We do **content marketing, copywriting, editorial services,**
and more. Email shuanthing.goh@gmail.com to enquire.

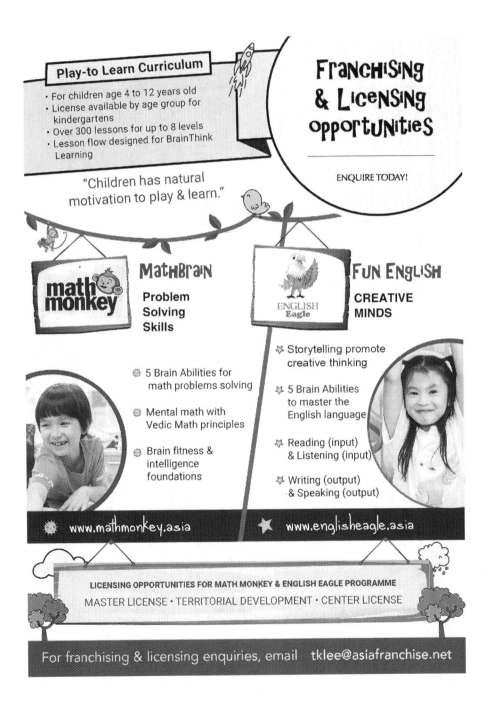

Play-to Learn Curriculum
- For children age 4 to 12 years old
- License available by age group for kindergartens
- Over 300 lessons for up to 8 levels
- Lesson flow designed for BrainThink Learning

"Children has natural motivation to play & learn."

FrANCHiSiNg & LiCeNSiNg opporTuNiTieS

ENQUIRE TODAY!

MathBrain

math monkey

Problem Solving Skills

- 5 Brain Abilities for math problems solving
- Mental math with Vedic Math principles
- Brain fitness & intelligence foundations

www.mathmonkey.asia

Fun English

ENGLISH Eagle

CREATIVE MINDS

- Storytelling promote creative thinking
- 5 Brain Abilities to master the English language
- Reading (input) & Listening (input)
- Writing (output) & Speaking (output)

www.englisheagle.asia

LICENSING OPPORTUNITIES FOR MATH MONKEY & ENGLISH EAGLE PROGRAMME
MASTER LICENSE · TERRITORIAL DEVELOPMENT · CENTER LICENSE

For franchising & licensing enquiries, email   tklee@asiafranchise.net

Printed in the United States
By Bookmasters